THE PERSONAL SECURITY HANDBOOK

THE PERSONAL SECURITY HANDBOOK

EFFECTIVE PROTECTION FOR YOUR HOME, YOUR CAR, YOUR FAMILY, YOURSELF

Consultant Editor
ALLAN DRAKE

Sphere Reference

A Marshall Edition
Conceived, edited and designed by
Marshall Editions Ltd
170 Piccadilly
London W1V 9DD

Editor
Barbara Horn

Art Editor
Roger Kohn

Associate Editor
Shelley Turner

Managing Editor
Ruth Binney

Production
Barry Baker
Janice Storr

Illustrators
János Márffy
Graham Rosewarne

Art Assistant
Brenda Breslan

Indexer
Donald Binney

First published 1987 by
Sphere Books Ltd
27 Wrights Lane
London W8 5TZ
Copyright © 1987
Marshall Editions Ltd

TRADE
MARK

SPHERE

Filmset in Century Old Style by Solecast Ltd, London.
Origination by Alpha Reprographics, Harefield, UK.
Printed and bound by Usines Brepols SA, Belgium.

CONSULTANT EDITOR

Allan Drake has a distinguished career in crime prevention. He was formerly an Inspector at the headquarters of the Metropolitan Police Crime Prevention Section, and subsequently Chief Inspector of the Home Office Crime Prevention Centre in Stafford. He is now a Crime Prevention Researcher for the British Telecom Investigation Department.

Acknowledgements

The publishers wish to thank the following for their invaluable assistance:
Frank Baker, Empire Security
Inspector Sue Best, Crime Prevention, Scotland Yard
Derek Cole, M.W. Insurance Brokers
Roger Crowther, Home and Overseas Insurance
Sgt Richard Dawe, Crime Prevention Officer, Heathrow Airport
David Gray, Fire Protection Association
Inspector John Houlgate, Crime Prevention, Scotland Yard
Catherine Stretton, St John Ambulance
Martin Wright, National Association of Victims Support Schemes

CONTENTS

INTRODUCTION

Every day the media report that homes are burgled, cars are stolen, bags are snatched and people are assaulted. No one, it seems is safe from the criminal – and the fear of crime grows even faster than crime itself.

The truth is that most crimes are casual offences committed, without forethought, when the opportunity arises. A kitchen window left open, a car door unlocked, an open handbag, a late-night walk down an unlit street – all are invitations to the criminal. The best way to protect yourself, your family and your property from being the victims of crime is to make sure that the opportunity doesn't arise in the first instance.

The Personal Security Handbook is your ally in the fight against crime. It shows you the kind of circumstances that invite or encourage crime, and the measures you can take to avoid or prevent them. These range from common-sense precautions to self-defence techniques, from simple locks to sophisticated alarm systems. It helps you to replace fear with awareness, vulnerability with confidence.

The Handbook is arranged in five sections:

● **Home Safe** explains how a burglar chooses his target and carries out his crime, and shows how you can keep him away and lock him out.

● **Vehicle Security** tells you what the car thief is looking for, and the products and procedures you can use to prevent him getting it.

● **The Wary Traveller** briefs you on securing the home you are leaving, protecting the things you take with you, and checking out the places you check in to.

● **Personal Safety** advises you on how to prevent putting yourself at risk at home, in your car, on public transport and in public places. It pays particular attention to the needs of women, children and the elderly, and illustrates some basic techniques of self-defence to use if you're attacked.

● **Teamwork** tells you more about the different members of the community who work together in the fight against crime, and explains how you can help too.

Throughout the book, drawings are used to illustrate the criminal's targets, and the best security products and procedures. DOs explained in the text are highlighted by numerals like this: ④; DON'Ts are shown by numerals like this: ❹.

Key points are regularly reviewed and emphasized. There are checklists to help you complete your own home security survey and compile an inventory for your household insurance. There is also advice on what to do if you are the victim of, or witness to, a crime.

REMEMBER!
Preventing crime is everyone's responsibility. This Handbook shows how it can be done.

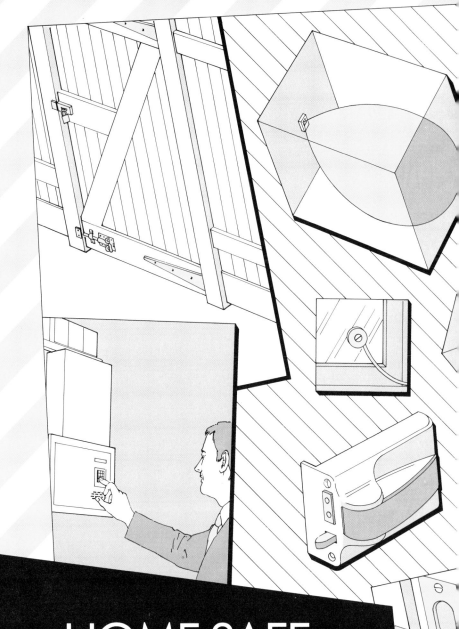

HOME SAFE

HOME
SAFE

HOME SAFE

Burglary is one of the most common crimes, and most of it is preventable. You can reduce the chances of your home being burgled by taking some basic security precautions.

Even if you think you do not have anything worth stealing, or are insured against the loss of, or damage to, your property, it is in your interests to protect your home. As a result of burglary, you are

FACTS ABOUT BURGLARY

● Between 80 and 90 per cent of burglars have no particular target in mind, but take advantage of the opportunities you give them. A thief may not even have a crime in mind when he is walking down the road, but an open ground floor window will prove irresistible if he knocks on the door and finds that no one is at home.

As many as 20 per cent of reported burglaries each year are committed without forcible entry: the burglar simply walks in through a door or climbs in through a window that is unlocked or open.
● The majority of residential burglaries are committed during the day, usually between 10am and 4pm, with the peak period in the afternoon, when a large proportion of homes are empty.
● Burglars prefer to break into unoccupied property because there is less likelihood of a confrontation with the occupier.
● Contrary to popular belief, violence during a burglary is rare. If he is disturbed or detected, the burglar's objective is to escape, preferably without being seen and without any physical contact.
● Vandalism is usually the work of juveniles; a burglar wants to get in and out of the premises with his stolen goods as quickly as possible.

PROTECTING YOUR HOME

Think of your home as a box within a box within a box. The outer box is the perimeter, the boundary of your property. The middle box is the shell of your home, its external walls and roof. The inner box is the interior of your house or flat. The best way to protect the three boxes that are your home is to use a three-stage strategy.

1 **Psychological deterrents**
Your prime objective is to discourage the burglar from breaching the perimeter and entering the grounds – to make him feel that your home is not an easy or suitable target (see pp. 20-5).

You have more control over this aspect of your security if you live in a house rather than in a block of flats.

2 **Physical deterrents**
If the first level of deterrent fails, the criminal will approach the middle box – the walls, windows and doors. You can deter him from attempting to break in by maintaining physical security at all possible points of entry (see pp. 14-17, 26-53).

3 **Defence**
In most cases the combination of the first two stages will succeed. However, you must still take steps to defend your valuable items if the thief is not deterred and manages to get into the inner box (see pp. 54-5, 62-5).

likely to suffer emotional distress over the loss of items of sentimental value, the feeling of invasion of your privacy, and also the considerable mess that thieves often make.

ALWAYS:

● Close and lock all windows and external doors when you go out (see pp. 34-44).

● Change your locks when you move into a new home or if you lose your keys (see pp. 28-9).

● Disguise a long absence by cancelling milk and paper deliveries, and getting a friend or neighbour to collect your post and give the home a lived-in look while you are away.

● Check the identity of any stranger before you take the chain or limiter off the door (see pp. 32-3).

● Notify the police of people behaving suspiciously around your property or that of your neighbour.

REMEMBER!
● *Most burglaries are not planned in advance.*
● *Many thieves get in through open windows or doors.*
● *With care and common sense you can minimize the chances of being burgled.*

POINTS of ENTRY 1

The illustrations on pages 14-17 show the areas around the different types of house that are the most vulnerable to a break-in. In flats, particularly those above ground level, almost all entries are through the front door.

Imagine that you have lost your key. Check all the possible entry points shown to see if you could get into your own home without it. Be sure to consider any upper storey windows that are accessible from flat roofs, climbable drain pipes or mature

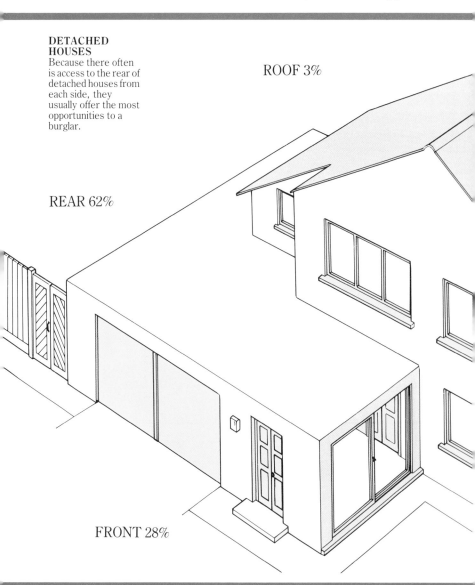

DETACHED HOUSES
Because there often is access to the rear of detached houses from each side, they usually offer the most opportunities to a burglar.

ROOF 3%

REAR 62%

FRONT 28%

trees. Even if you can't get in without causing any damage, it's very likely that you will just need to break a pane of glass in a window, operate a catch, open the window and climb through. If you *can* find a way in, the burglar certainly *will*.

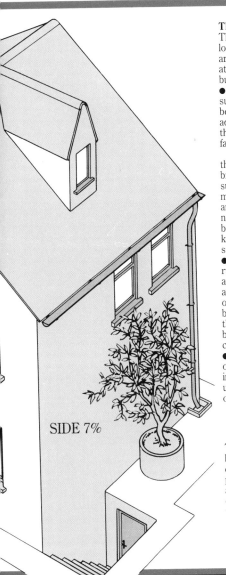

SIDE 7%

The environment
The situation and location of a building are factors in attracting or deterring burglars.

● Houses in urban and suburban areas may be situated in rows of adjoining streets so that their fronts are facing each other.

A burglar knows that if he attempts to break into the front of such a building he might be spotted by an observant neighbour or passer-by – a phenomenon known as natural surveillance.

● Detached houses in rural areas tend to be away from the road and a long way from other houses. The burglar can work at the front of these buildings with far less chance of being seen.

● There is much less opportunistic burglary in rural areas than in urban and suburban ones.

The percentage of break-ins that occur at each point varies from place to place and according to the type of house, but the figures shown are a general guide.

POINTS of ENTRY 1

REMEMBER!
● *If you* can *break into your own home, a thief* will.

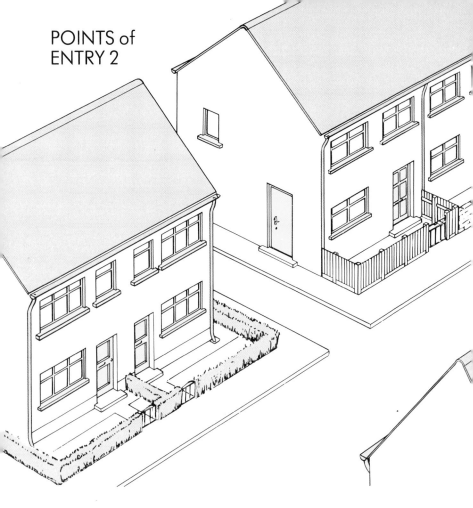

OTHER TYPES OF HOUSE

TERRACED HOUSES

● Terraced houses with back-to-back gardens are the least prone to burglary. The difficulty of gaining access to the rear of the buildings makes them less attractive to thieves.

● Terraces that back on to an alley or road are more vulnerable.

SEMI-DETACHED HOUSES

● Semis are potentially more vulnerable than terraces because there usually is side access to the back of the building.

● Semi-detached houses that are linked together by garages, and therefore do not have a side access, are in the same category as terraced houses.

The environment

● Terraced and semi-detached houses are usually in rows of adjoining streets in cities, towns, suburbs and villages, and so benefit from natural surveillance.

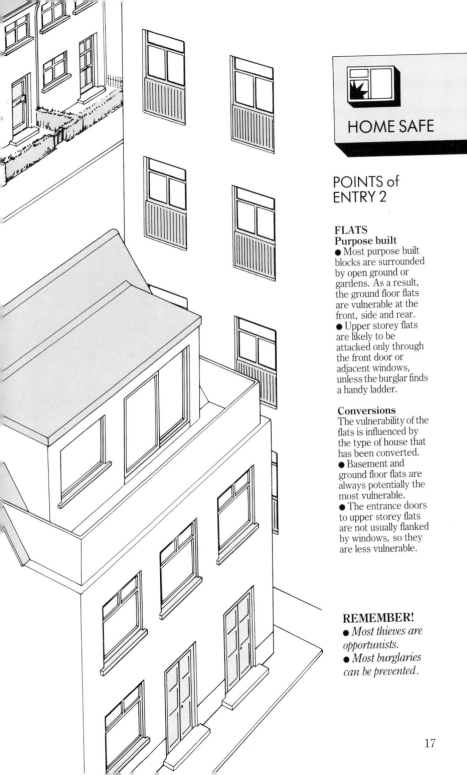

POINTS of ENTRY 2

FLATS
Purpose built
● Most purpose built blocks are surrounded by open ground or gardens. As a result, the ground floor flats are vulnerable at the front, side and rear.
● Upper storey flats are likely to be attacked only through the front door or adjacent windows, unless the burglar finds a handy ladder.

Conversions
The vulnerability of the flats is influenced by the type of house that has been converted.
● Basement and ground floor flats are always potentially the most vulnerable.
● The entrance doors to upper storey flats are not usually flanked by windows, so they are less vulnerable.

REMEMBER!
● *Most thieves are opportunists.*
● *Most burglaries can be prevented.*

17

ANATOMY of a BURGLARY

The following example is typical of the way in which many burglaries are committed.

The burglar
He is between the ages of 18 and 25. He works alone, and doesn't carry any house-breaking tools.

The time and place
It is mid-afternoon on a weekday in a street of semi-detached houses in suburbia. The weather is dry.

The approach

1 The burglar walks along the road looking for signs that a house may be unoccupied: milk still on the step or a newspaper in the door.

2 He looks for easy access to the rear of the house – no fencing or a low gate.

3 He prefers a place where there aren't any houses opposite from which he could be seen. He also likes a house that has a lot of foliage in front to hide his movements (see pp. 20-1).

● He looks round to make sure he's not being watched.

4 He knocks at the door. If the door is answered, the burglar makes an excuse and moves on.

● If there is no reply, he tries the front door and has a quick look for a hidden key (see pp. 28-9).

5 If the front windows are hidden from view, he tries them. He would be delighted to find an open window, but will be quite happy to find one without a lock (see pp. 42-3).

● If he doesn't get in at the front, the burglar moves quickly to the back of the house.

The entry

6 The burglar tries the back doors and windows. He finds a large side-hung casement window divided into small panes. It's secured by a cockspur handle, but there's no lock.

● He finds a brick in the garden, and uses it to break the small pane nearest the handle (see pp. 48-9).

7 He reaches in to release the latch, opens the window and climbs in.

8 The burglar looks for a quick and easy way out. He checks whether the keys have been left in the back or front door. If not, he checks all the hiding places for keys in the kitchen and hall.

If he doesn't find the keys, he will have to leave the way he came in.

At work

● The burglar starts at the top of the house. He works as quickly as possible and doesn't worry about making a mess.

9 He goes to the main bedroom first. He takes any cash or jewellery on view, then empties all the drawers.

10 He checks all the shelves and the pockets of clothing in the wardrobes.

11 He looks under the rug, under the bed and under the mattress.

● He takes camera equipment, radios and expensive clocks.

12 He puts the stolen goods into his pockets, a bag or even a suitcase or briefcase he has found in the house.

13 He then repeats the performance in the other bedrooms. He will even take the cash from the children's money boxes.

14 He goes downstairs. He empties drawers and shelves in desks and cabinets in the lounge and dining room. He takes money and any small silver or porcelain items. He

might also take the television or video recorder.

15 He searches the kitchen. He's likely to find the money to pay the milkman or paperboy in the old pot in the cupboard.

The exit

● He leaves by the back door if the key is available, or climbs out of the window. He looks round quickly to make sure that no one will see him, and walks away.

● The whole episode has taken no more than 10 minutes.

HOME SAFE

ANATOMY of a BURGLARY

REMEMBER!

● *Most burglars are opportunists.*
● *Most burglaries are committed in 10 minutes or less.*
● *Most burglaries can be prevented.*

KEEP AWAY! 1

The way you manage your immediate environment can provide a deterrent or an invitation to a criminal. Obviously a burglar does not want to be seen breaking into a house, so he will be reluctant to approach the front of the building that is overlooked by houses opposite, or in a road where there are frequent passers-by. This natural surveillance is an effective deterrent only if the building is clearly visible.

DETERRENTS

1 An alarm bell box on the wall of the house, whether or not you have an alarm system.
2 Neighbourhood Watch street signs and window stickers (see pp.146-7).
3 Property Marking Scheme window stickers (see pp. 66-7).
4 Beware of the Dog plaque on the gate.
5 Net curtains in windows that face the road.
6 Position prickly plants, such as roses or holly, in front of the windows below sill level as a further deterrent.
7 Fit exterior lights and have them operated by a time switch.
8 Use anti-climb paint on drainpipes.
9 Turn illuminated faces on electrical equipment away from the window.
10 Keep a trained guard dog.

External signs that you are security conscious can discourage a burglar from even approaching your property.

NATURAL SURVEILLANCE

11 Do not obscure the front of the building with a high wall, fence or hedge, which allows the burglar to work on the front door and windows with little chance of being seen and detected.

12 Don't plant tall shrubs near the front door and windows.

13 Make sure that an enclosed porch has some glass panelling so that the front door remains visible.

REMEMBER!

● *A dog is a deterrent only when it is at home and if it barks when strangers approach.*

● *You can buy a recording of a dog barking that is activated when the doorbell is depressed.*

● *Electronic equipment with an illuminated face, such as a video recorder, is easily spotted: keep it turned away from the window.*

● *Don't rely on visual deterrents or alarm systems alone: make sure your property is physically secure.*

KEEP AWAY! 2

PERIMETER BARRIERS

A wall or fence blocking the side entrance is an ideal way to deter a burglar from attempting to get round to the back of the building. However, if any of your neighbours is not security conscious, a burglar might gain access to the back of your building through his side entrance. Your home is also vulnerable if any of the perimeter abuts on open land. For maximum security you need a barrier around the sides and

Walls
A solid brick or stone wall to the maximum height allowed by the local authority is the best perimeter barrier.
● Its advantage over other barriers is that an intruder cannot easily breach it, but would have to climb up and over.
● Its disadvantage is that it is more expensive than the others.

● Avoid decorative features, such as projecting bricks and alcoves for plants or ornaments, which provide ready-made footholds for an intruder to use to scale the wall.
● Add a further level of security by topping the wall with a trellis and training climbing roses along it.
● You must not top your wall with broken glass or barbed wire without the consent of the local authority.

Iron railings
Vertical iron railings provide a reasonably secure perimeter barrier and still allow natural surveillance where this exists.
● The rails must be set sufficiently close together to avoid gaps through which an intruder could squeeze.
● Horizontal rails must not be added in a way that would assist climbing.
● Railings can also be used to extend the height of brick walls.

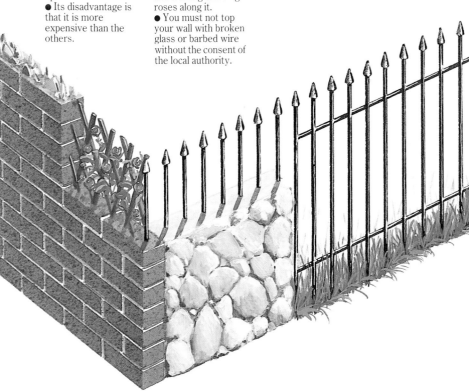

back of your property. In areas where there is no natural surveillance at the front, use a perimeter barrier all around the property.

Gates

The main weakness in a perimeter barrier is usually the gate because it is designed to be opened. The way in which it is constructed and locked are important to the security of the barrier.

● All gates, whether for pedestrians or motor vehicles, should be the same height as the perimeter barrier, and have only the minimum clearance at the bottom.

● Use a stout, solid wooden gate in a wall or solid fence barrier.

● Fit a side gate with a five-lever mortise lock or a rim deadlock (see pp. 36-7), or a close shackle padlock and hasp (see pp. 40-1) about halfway down the inside.

● Fit the non-locking leaf of double gates with a strong bottom bolt. Fit a top bolt, too, if the gates are not as tall as the barrier and are set under a lintel.

● Wrought iron gates, like railings, must be designed so that they cannot be used as a climbing frame.

● Secure a wrought iron side gate with a close shackle padlock and locking bolt.

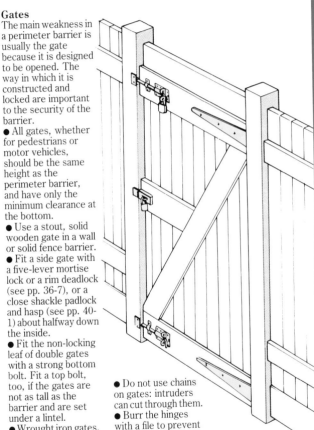

● Do not use chains on gates: intruders can cut through them.
● Burr the hinges with a file to prevent gates being lifted off.

Wooden fences
● Close board wooden fencing offers little security. A burglar can easily cut a hole in it large enough to gain access.

● Paddock fencing does not provide any protection, no matter how high it is. More rails only mean more steps on the ladder.

REMEMBER!
● *Plan fences and railings so that they are not climbable.*
● *Check the permitted height for perimeter fences and gates with the local authority.*

23

KEEP AWAY! 3

The following means of discouraging intruders are optional. They can contribute to home security, but they are not substitutes for the basic forms of protection described elsewhere in this chapter. Whether or not you use them will depend on both your circumstances and your preferences.

DISCOURAGING APPROACH

WATCH-DOGS

Most dogs, including mongrels, have natural territorial instincts and a protective attitude toward their human family. They can be trained to guard the home.

Alarm dogs

Any dog that barks at the approach of strangers is a good alarm. However, for your peace of mind, and that of your neighbours, the dog must be taught to stop barking on command.

Size is not important, since an alarm dog is a psychological deterrent – it is expected to frighten intruders, not tackle them.

Terriers make excellent alarm dogs.

Guard dogs

Some large dogs, such as the Great Dane and the Mastiff, deter intruders just by their size.

These and other medium-sized and large dogs can be trained to defend you and your home against attack, as well as to raise the alarm.

Alsatians (German Shepherds), Dobermans and Rottweilers consistently display the characteristics that make good guard dogs.

Patrol dogs

Patrol dogs are not suitable as domestic watch-dogs: they are too dangerous.

These dogs are trained to attack on sight and must be in the care of professional handlers at all times.

Points to consider

● Dogs that are essentially pets are not a physical deterrent to intruders.

● A guard dog should be bought young and trained by a professional instructor, who will show you how to handle it.

A poorly trained guard dog might harm innocent people, and is a liability.

● Your choice of dog will be influenced by where you live.

Large dogs need plenty of space, and it is unfair to keep them in a flat or a house without a garden. Small and medium-sized dogs adapt better to urban conditions.

● A dog is no substitute for a conventional alarm system (see pp. 50-61), particularly if it goes with you or into a kennel when you are on holiday.

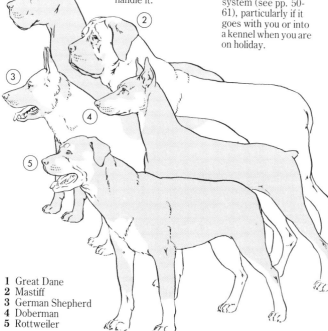

1 Great Dane
2 Mastiff
3 German Shepherd
4 Doberman
5 Rottweiler

KEEP AWAY! 3

GEESE

Geese are highly territorial and honk furiously, making a terrific racket, at the approach of strangers.

They are also physical deterrents. A few large, angry geese hissing and flapping their wings, are an intimidating sight. They will chase, and even peck, anyone who does not retreat.

However, geese can be quite noisy even when there is no cause for alarm, and they make a mess of the lawn. They are usually kept only in rural areas.

DISCOURAGING ENTRY

1 You should fit locks to any windows that can be reached from drainpipes (see pp. 14-19, 42-7). You can also deter intruders from attempting to climb the pipes.

2 Replace metal drainpipes with plastic ones. Most plastic pipes are not strong enough to support a climber. They are likely to pull away from the wall, bringing an intruder to the ground.

3 Grow prickly, thorny plants or thick, impenetrable shrubs around the base of pipes.

4 Build a cement fillet between drainpipes and walls to prevent a burglar getting a grip around the back of the pipe. Check with a builder that this will not cause damp in your walls.

5 Place a spiked metal collar around each drainpipe about 2.5 m (8 ft) up. This is a visual as well as a physical deterrent.

6 Paint drainpipes with anti-climb paint. It comes in several colours and remains sticky for several years.

To avoid accidental damage to clothing, apply the paint to pipes starting about 2.5 m (8 ft) above ground level and continuing for 2.5 m (8 ft). One section of paint is enough, even for houses of more than two storeys.

The only minor disadvantage is that insects tend to get stuck to the paint, which can be unsightly.

REMEMBER!

● *Display a 'Beware of the Dog' sign even if your dog isn't dangerous.*

● *Don't get a dog for security purposes unless you are a dog-lover and the animal fits in with your, or your family's, lifestyle.*

● *A watch-dog is not a substitute for an alarm system.*

● *Anti-climb measures are no substitute for upstairs window locks.*

IN the LIMELIGHT

At night the darkness reduces the advantages of natural surveillance and shields the criminal. Exterior lighting on your home helps to redress the balance and makes the burglar feel he is likely to be detected.

If your house has a small front garden, the light from an adjacent street lamp might illuminate the front of the house well enough, but the front porch will probably still require extra lighting, and the sides and back certainly will.

HOUSE

Porch lighting
● Makes an intruder visible.
● Enables you to identify a caller at night without opening the door by using a door viewer, window or closed circuit TV.
● Should illuminate the entire porch and not cast shadows.
1 Can be positioned on a side wall to give better coverage.
2 Can be positioned over the door so that it also illuminates the approach path.

Front elevation lighting
3 Can be fitted to the top of the wall (or to the garden wall) to illuminate the garden area surrounding your property.
● Should not cast shadows near the windows, which would provide a burglar with cover to open or attack them.
● Should not shine into the windows, which would prevent you from seeing into the garden.
● Can be mounted on corner wall brackets to illuminate two flanks.

Inside lighting
● Should be left on in a downstairs room with the curtains closed.
● Should never be left on only in the hall. Any burglar knows that no one spends an evening just in the hall.
● Can be linked to automatic time-switches.

GARAGE
You need security lighting on your garage if it is not well-lit by street or house lights.
4 It can illuminate the area between the garage and the house, allowing you safer access as well as deterring burglars.
● It provides a lighted area in which to unload your car.
● It should not be positioned above an 'up and over' door because it will be obscured when the door is open.
● It should be equipped with switches at both the house and garage.

DRIVES AND PATHS
If you have a long path or drive that does not benefit from the lighting on the building, set small lighting bollards at its edges at regular intervals.

Place the first lights about 6 m (20 ft) inside the gate to avoid disturbing drivers on the road.

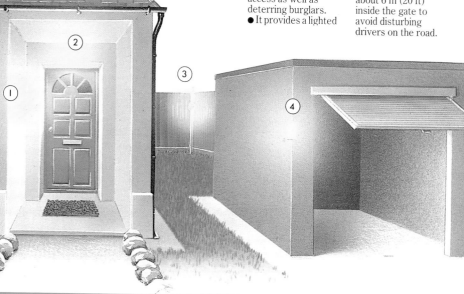

By using interior lighting sensibly you can give an unoccupied house an occupied look and thus also help to deter intruders.

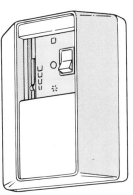

Automatic time-switch

Photo-electric cell

IN the LIMELIGHT

Automatic time-switch
This simple-to-fit device will turn your lights on and off at pre-set times. You have to reset it to take account of seasonal changes in the length of day.

Solar dial time-switch
A more advanced version of the simple time-switch, this device is programmed for the seasonal changes in day length.

Photo-electric cell
Not a time-switch, this sophisticated mechanism measures the intensity of natural light.

When the light falls below a certain level, the cell automatically switches on the electric lights. It switches off the lights when daylight returns.

It takes account of seasonal variations and fluctuations in the quality of daylight due to weather conditions.

Passive infra-red detector
This device automatically switches on a light when it detects the infra-red radiation emitted by a living body. It is useful in places where you do not want to leave lights on throughout the night.

CONTROLS FOR EXTERIOR LIGHTING

Your exterior lighting will be most effective as a deterrent if it operates whether or not you are at home. Obviously you can control the lighting with a simple on/off switch, but you have to be at home to do so. That is inconvenient not only when you are away on holiday, but also during winter months when darkness falls before most people are home from work. There are several controls that overcome this problem. The cost varies according to the complexity of the system, but all are excellent deterrents.

REMEMBER!
● *Make sure that all doors are properly lit.*
● *You can get advice on all types of external security and design of installations from your local electricity board or the National Inspection Council for Electrical Installation Contracting.*
● *Don't link automatic timing devices to televisions: this creates a fire risk.*

Whatever the level of physical security in your home, it will occasionally be breached when you open the door to allow someone to come inside. It is imperative that only people who have your permission enter your home. The various methods by which you ensure this are known in the security industry as access control.

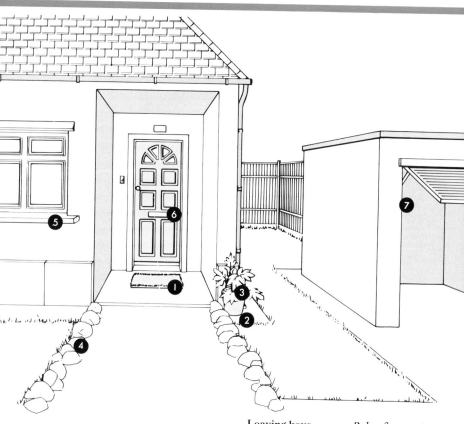

KEY SECURITY

The simplest form of access control is a mechanical lock in a door. You and other inhabitants of the house have keys, and you may give keys to other people who have your authority to pass through the door. You wouldn't give a thief permission to enter your home, so don't give him the keys.

Leaving keys outside
The burglar knows all the hiding places people use to leave keys for each other, and he'll check them all to save himself the trouble of breaking in.

NEVER leave keys in any of these places:
1 Under the doormat.
2 Under a flowerpot.
3 In a flowerpot.
4 Under a stone in the path.
5 Stuck under the window ledge.
6 Hanging inside the door on a piece of string that can be pulled through the letter box.
7 Just inside an unlocked garage or shed.

Keys inside
If a burglar manages to break into your home through a window, the first thing he will look for is a route out through a door. It's easier to carry the goods out through a door than a window and he needs a quick escape route if he's disturbed.

Don't make it easy for him.
1 Don't leave the keys in the locks of exterior doors when the house is unoccupied.
2 Don't leave keys in obvious places like cupboards or hooks by the door.
● If possible, take all exterior door keys with you.

Carrying keys
You might lose your keys and not realize you have lost them until several hours later. Don't make them a gift for a dishonest person.
● Don't have your name or address on your keys.
● Change your locks as soon as possible.

Registered keys
Most keys can be copied in any high street, but some keys can be replaced only by the manufacturer.

A specimen of the owner's signature is taken when the lock is sold and must be matched before a replacement key will be supplied.

Moving house
When you move house, you will be given the keys, but you don't know how many other sets there may be. To be secure, change the locks.

ACCESS CONTROL 1

REMEMBER!
● *Be absolutely sure of the honesty of anyone to whom you lend your keys.*
● *Don't put your name or address on spare keys you leave with a friend or neighbour.*
● *If you can think of places to hide your keys outdoors, so can the criminal.*

ACCESS CONTROL 2

KEEPER AT THE GATE

To be secure you need to exercise control over people other than keyholders who come to your door. It is essential that you can identify the caller before you decide to open the door. If you live in a house or in a ground floor flat you may be able to get a good view of a caller through a window. Even so, you might not know the person and need to see identification. The following devices enable you to do this safely.

Door chain
A door chain allows the door to be opened only a little way, so you can check proof of identification or sign for and receive a letter or package without admitting the caller.

It gives you an immediate psychological advantage and offers good resistance to a kick against the door. You should use a chain even if you have a door viewer.

● Choose the strongest chain you can find.

● For secure anchorage use screws that are at least 30 mm (1³⁄₁₆ in) long. Buy them separately if the ones supplied are too short.

● Angle the screws into the woodwork in different directions.

● Put a note inside the door near the chain to remind you to use it.

Some police forces supply brightly coloured stickers: ask your local Crime Prevention Officer.

Door limiter
A door limiter serves the same purpose as a chain, but works on a sliding rod principle. It probably offers a little more resistance than a chain to a physical attack on the door.

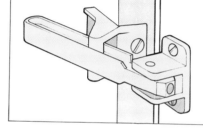

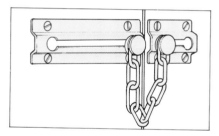

Door viewer
If you can't get a good view of a caller through a window, a door viewer is essential. This small lens fits into the door like a miniature telescope so that you can see out from the inside. The wide-angled model provides a 180° field of vision.

You can fit a door viewer yourself if you are a DIY enthusiast, or have it installed professionally. Be sure to take account of the varying heights of the occupants when positioning it in the door.

Audio entry system
A speaker panel located near the outside of the front door is linked to a telephone handset or microphone device inside to permit two-way speech.

This system is popular in blocks of flats to control access through a common entrance door. Each flat is equipped with the system and a remote control that releases the electricity operated lock.

It is not recommended as a sole means of access control. Each flat should also be equipped with a door viewer and chain or limiter.

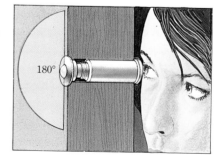

ACCESS CONTROL 2

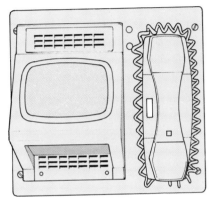

Audio-visual entry system

The ability to see your callers as well as speak to them greatly enhances your security.

The audio-visual entry system incorporates a closed circuit television camera in or near the external speech panel. The picture is relayed to a monitor near the telephone handset inside the home.

Some systems are designed to use a spare channel on your TV set, so that if you are watching it and the doorbell rings, you can change channels to see your caller.

Hall porter/ security officer

Usually employed only in blocks of luxury flats, a hall porter or security officer does not allow anyone to get farther than the common entrance hall without establishing his or her right to do so.

Usually this means using an internal telephone system to contact the occupant the caller is supposed to be visiting.

You should also have a door viewer and chain to check the caller's identity.

REMEMBER!

● *While your door is open, your security is breached.*

● *You do not have to open the door if you do not like the look of the caller or are not absolutely sure of his or her identity.*

● *Light the area in front of the door during hours of darkness and in dark corridors.*

● *Always use your door viewer and chain.*

BURGLARY BY ARTIFICE

There is one kind of burglar who can defeat all your physical defences by simply knocking on your door and persuading you to invite him in. He's the con-man and his crime is called burglary by artifice.

The con-man operates in so many different ways and has so many new stories to fool the unwary that it is impossible to

The official
The burglar calls at your door and claims to be an official from the electricity, gas or water board or the local council.

The 'electricity board official' may ask you, for example, to stand by the fuse box and turn the power on and off while he goes around the house checking the circuit.

The 'gas board official' might ask you to watch the meter outside while he checks your appliances.

The 'water board official' may ask you to turn the taps in the kitchen while he checks the flow upstairs.

The 'council official' may want to measure the rooms for rating purposes.

The salesman or antiques buyer
The phoney salesman may offer to measure your rooms for a free estimate for fitted carpets or fitted furniture. The bedroom is his main target.

The 'antiques buyer' will want to browse around your home looking for interesting pieces to buy.

Adult and child
Don't be fooled by this innocent-looking couple. They might throw a ball into your back garden, then knock at your door and ask if the child can go and look for it. While you show the child into the garden, the adult stays in the house and steals.

Reversing roles, the child might ask to use the lavatory urgently. The adult remains downstairs with you while the child steals from the bedrooms upstairs.

Chimney sweep
This trick is less common now because of the decline in popularity of open solid fuel fires. The bogus sweep asks you to go into the garden and tell him when you see his brush coming out of the chimney. While alone in the house, he steals.

OTHER DECEPTIONS

The workman
He will call at your door and tell you that your chimney stack needs repointing or your roof requires new slates or tiles, or that he can re-tarmac your driveway. His estimate of costs will be very attractive, but he will ask for an advance to buy the materials. After you have given him the money, you won't see him again.

The salesman
He will show you a catalogue or samples of attractively priced goods, but will ask for a deposit with your order. If you give him the money, he will disappear and the goods will never arrive.

give a comprehensive list of the rules he uses. However, here are some of his most common – and successful – tricks. In each case, the caller's intention is to steal your property.

PROTECT YOURSELF

● Always use the door chain or limiter when you answer the door.
● Don't be lulled into a false sense of security because the caller is wearing an official-looking uniform.
● Insist on seeing his official identity card. If you don't know what one looks like, drop into your local showrooms to see a specimen of each kind.
● Keep the chain or limiter on while you check the identification.
● If you still have *any* doubt after seeing the card, close the door and keep the caller waiting outside while you telephone the appropriate authority to check his identity.
● If you don't have a telephone, tell the caller to come back when you have made an appointment through official channels.
● If the caller claims it is an emergency, you should expect to see an official van and other workmen nearby.
● Electricity, gas and water board authorities and local councils will make special arrangements when their officials need to call on blind people. Consult them or your Crime Prevention Officer.
● Don't leave any stranger alone in any part of your home.
● Be suspicious of two people calling together claiming to be officials, salesmen or workmen.
● Never part with money until you are certain of the credentials of the salesman or workman.

Take details of the company he represents or his address and ask him to return at a later date while you think about his offer. In the meantime you can check his identity.

Genuine salesmen and workmen will return, the thief is unlikely to take the risk.

● If you are suspicious about anybody calling at your door, play safe: call the police.

ACCESS CONTROL 3

REMEMBER!

● *Always use the door viewer and chain or limiter.*
● *Don't let strangers in your home until you are absolutely sure of their identity.*
● *Not all criminals are men: women and children commit burglaries and deceptions too.*
● *You don't have to let anyone into your home if you don't like the look of them, even if they have bona fide references.*

DOORS

You need to consider very carefully the security your front door offers. It may be your only door if you live in a flat, or the door by which you leave if you live in a house. As a result, it can be secured only by locks when the house is unoccupied. Front doors offer varying standards of security, depending on their construction.

Ideally, back and side doors should be to the same standard as the front door,

Panelled door

Two types of glazed door

EXTERNAL DOORS

SOLID DOORS

The most effective door is constructed of solid hardwood or solid hardcore at least 45 mm (1¾ in) thick, and without any glazed areas.

It can resist a strong physical attack and is ideal for fitting good quality security hardware.

Hardcore is composed of hardwood chippings bonded together. It gives the same protection as hardwood at a much lower cost.

Panelled doors

Doors with rebated wooden panels look quite strong, but often are very weak and vulnerable to a hefty kick or a hacksaw blade.

You can increase the security of a panelled door with 16-gauge steel sheeting, which can be fitted to the inside of the door and painted to match the decor. Your Crime Prevention Officer or a locksmith can advise you on the correct way to fit this.

GLAZED DOORS

Doors that have glazed areas are likely to be attacked by an intruder who will try to reach the latch on the inside.

Very few burglars break glass in order to climb through it. They are too likely to get cut on the jagged edges when they are trying to carry goods or escape.

You can further discourage anyone from attempting entry through glass.
● Have glazing in the upper part of the door only (see Access to locks, right).
● Line the bottom panels of glass with 16-gauge steel sheeting.
● Fit a strong ornamental grille on the inside of the door. It can be hinged on one side with a lock on the other so that you can open it to clean the glass.

Patio doors

The main security risk in sliding doors with either a wooden or aluminium frame is the fitting.

The doors must fit so that there is no free play. If there is, a burglar can lift them out of position.

Install patio door locks (see pp. 38-41).

Large areas of glass are less likely to be broken by a burglar than smaller ones.

French doors

French doors usually open outward.

An intruder can easily and quietly break the small panes of glass to reach the latch. Fit locking bolts (see pp. 38-41) to keep him out.

because a thief is most likely to attempt to enter through them. However, unlike the front door, they can be strengthened with internal bolts.

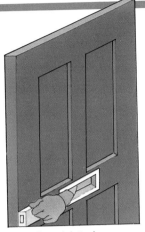

Entry through letterbox

small dog. If a small child could get through your pet flap, you are at risk.

DOORS

INTERNAL DOORS

In most modern homes internal doors are of hollow construction. They can easily be broken through and it is not worth fitting them with locks.

Older homes may have stronger doors, perhaps with good locks. However, unless the house is alarmed, don't lock internal doors when the premises are unoccupied.

Once inside, the burglar can work unseen and the damage he causes breaking through doors as he goes from room to room may be greater than the value of the property stolen.

CELLAR FLAPS

If you have external cellar flaps, check that the wood is in good condition.

You can improve your security by lining the flaps with 16-gauge steel sheeting.

Secure the flaps with two padlocks and bar (see pp. 40-41).

REMEMBER!

● *Refit patio doors that allow free play.*
● *Your door frames must be as good as your doors.*
● *Fix a guard plate or grille inside the door around a letter box that is too close to the lock.*

Access to locks

Most burglars will break glass so that they can reach in to open the latch. Make sure your lock meets these criteria:
● It can be opened only with a key.
● There is at least 40 cm (16 in) between the lock and the letter box. If there is not, fit a guard plate or metal letter basket inside the door.

DOOR FRAMES

Make sure that all your door frames are in good condition and properly secured, and fit tight to the surrounding masonry.

Hardwood frames provide better security than softwood frames.

When you have added security safeguards, such as steel sheeting, that increase the weight of a door with only two hinges, fit an extra pair of 10-cm (4-in) long steel hinges halfway down the stile.

OTHER DOORS

Doors that are ledged and braced or framed, ledged and braced provide no security at all and should be replaced.

Pet flaps

Pet flaps should be large enough only to allow entry by a cat or

LOCKS 1

The kind of lock you choose will depend partly on your preference and partly on the construction of your door. All your security locks should comply with British Standard (BS) 3621.

- The bolt must have a throw of at least 14mm ($9/16$ in).
- The bolt must be able to withstand 113 kg (250 lb) end pressure.
- The bolt must pass an anti-drill test.
- The locking plates must be able to withstand 1,360 kg (3,000 lb) pressure applied to the side of the closed door.
- The bolt must be deadlocking – that is, it can be withdrawn into the lockcase only by using a key.
- The lock must be manufactured with at least 1,000 key variations.

A burglar cannot open a deadlock without a key even if he can reach it through a broken window or panel, and he cannot force the bolt back by manipulating an object between the door and the frame.

Locks that have been approved by the British Standards Institution (BSI) carry the 'kite' mark. Your Crime Prevention Officer can advise you about other locks that meet or exceed the standards but have not been submitted to the BSI.

TYPES OF LOCK

Mortise lock
A mortise lock fits into a recess cut into the locking stile (leading edge) of the door so that only the faceplate and keyhole are visible. It can include a handle for convenience.

The mechanism is operated by a key that acts either on flat levers in the lockcase or a cylinder containing pin tumblers. Keys for lever locks are flat; keys for cylinder locks have a round stem.

The metal plate into which the bolt shoots when it is extended is called the striking plate. It should have a box compartment to protect the bolt against an attack with a jemmy. Most BS locks come with a box striking plate.

The lock may have a square, hook or clutch bolt. The latter two hook into the striking plate box.

They are particularly recommended for french doors because they are less likely to spring when the doors are pulled or pushed.

Do not use a mortise lock on a door that is less than 45 mm ($1\frac{3}{4}$ in) thick. The amount of wood that needs to be removed in order to fit the lock will weaken the door around the lock.

The stile should be at least 75 mm (3 in) wide. There are specially designed locks for narrower stiles.

Mortise latch-lock
This mortise lock, also called a mortise sashlock, incorporates a latch and handle.

It gives you the convenience of being able to open and close the door without a key when you are indoors and deadlock it when you go out. It is recommended mainly for side and back doors.

Rim lock
A rim lock is a deadlock that fits on the inside surface of the door. It can be used on doors that are less than 45 mm ($1\frac{3}{4}$ in) thick.

The lock is usually operated by a cylinder mechanism.

Night latches
Don't confuse a night latch with a rim lock. A night latch does not deadlock, so a burglar can force it open without a key. It provides no security.

FITTING LOCKS
Fitting a rim lock involves making a round hole of a specific size through the door to hold the lock barrel.

It is not difficult if you have reasonable DIY skills and follow the instructions carefully and exactly.

Fitting a mortise lock involves some carpentry skills in chiselling out a new mortise.

If you are replacing a substandard lock with one conforming to BS 3621, you might find one that requires only a slight enlargement of the existing mortise.

In both instances be careful not to remove too much wood, which would result in an ill-fitting lock and a weaker door.

COST
Mortise locks are less expensive than rim locks because they are concealed in the door, and so do not have to be made to look attractive.

BUYING LOCKS
If you are buying and fitting your own locks, you need the following information about the door.
● Thickness.
● Depth of the stile.
● Material.
● The direction in which it opens: inward or outward.
● Whether the locking edge is the right or the left.
● Whether it is rebated and dimensions of the rebate.

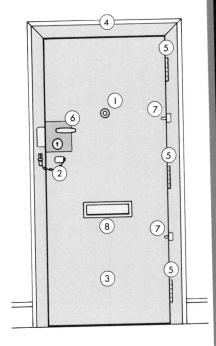

REMEMBER!
● *Check that all your external doors have deadlocks.*
● *Make sure every external lock is fitted with a box striking plate.*

Front door
The illustration shows a typical front door with its lock and security devices in postition.

Alternatively, you could have a rim lock in place of the mortise, if you prefer a slam action, and move the mortise two-thirds of the way down the door for extra security.

1 Door viewer
2 Door chain or limiter
3 Solid door
4 Strong door frame

5 Steel hinges
6 Mortise lock
7 Hinge bolts
8 Letter box 40 cm (16 in) from lock

LOCKS 2

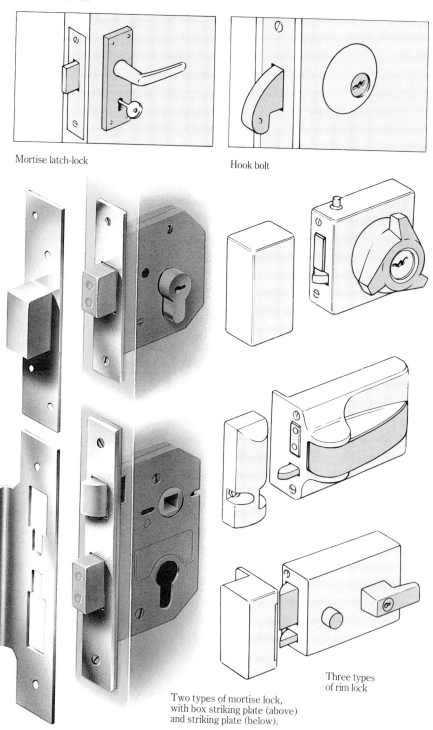

Mortise latch-lock

Hook bolt

Two types of mortise lock,
with box striking plate (above)
and striking plate (below).

Three types
of rim lock

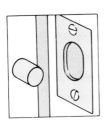

Hinge bolt

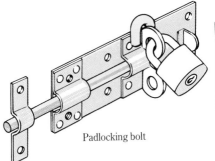

Padlocking bolt

HOME SAFE

LOCKS 2

Sliding grille lock

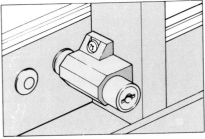

Patio door lock

Medium duty padlock

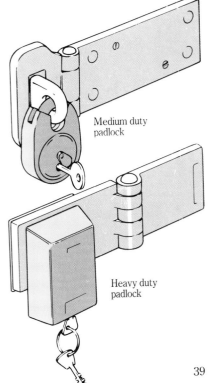

Heavy duty padlock

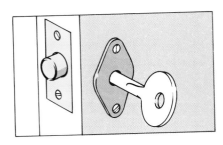

Mortise bolt

LOCKS 3

Mortise and rim locks are not the only types of lock available, nor are they suitable to all types of door. There are other devices you can use to increase your level of security.

BOLTS

HINGE BOLTS

Hinge bolts are metal cylinders fixed on the hinge edge of the door that fit into holes on the frame when the door is closed.

They protect the hinge side of the door from being forced or lifted. They are essential on outward-opening doors, such as french doors, because the hinges are on the outside and vulnerable to attack.

You must fit hinge bolts in pairs, one below the top hinge and the other above the bottom hinge.

SURFACE BOLTS

As their name suggests, surface bolts are screwed onto the surface of the door. They shoot into a staple on the door frame.

● The barrel bolt runs in a continuous guide.
● The tower bolt is exposed except for two small guides.

Surface bolts can be positioned horizontally or vertically and are suitable only for solid doors; a burglar can break through a glass or panelled door and easily withdraw a bolt.

● Fit two bolts, one at the top part of the door, the other at the bottom part.
● Fit one bolt horizontally into the locking frame and the other vertically into the top frame, floor or sill.

The staple is vulnerable to physical pressure on the door.
● Use the biggest screws the staple will take.
● Fit a metal strap over the staple and secure it with two or more woodscrews on each side.

Espagnolette bolts

An espagnolette consists of two vertical bolts, one covering the top half of the door, the other covering the bottom half.

The bolts are connected and operated by a central lock. When the key is turned, it shoots or retracts both bolts simultaneously.

● Fit espagnolette bolts to metal-framed side, back and french doors.

MORTISE BOLT

A mortise bolt fits into the door in the same way as a mortise lock.

It is a deadlock and therefore suitable for glass or thin wood-panelled doors, since an intruder who breaks through the door cannot release it without a key.

● Fit each door of a double door with two vertical mortise bolts, one shooting into the top frame, the other into the floor or sill.

Patio door lock

This cross between a surface and a mortise bolt is designed for aluminium-framed sliding doors that cannot be fitted with a regular mortise lock.

A surface-mounted bolt on one door shoots into a mortise on the other and is locked with a key.

It prevents the door frames from being lifted off the track or the door being opened by breaking the glass.

Fit one lock at the top of the post and one at the bottom. When buying the locks, ask for them to be keyed alike for convenience.

OTHER LOCKS

Padlocks

Padlocks come in different qualities appropriate to the risk they are designed to protect.

Use them to secure, or increase security on, garage and shed doors and garden gates.

Choose a medium duty padlock with a hardened shackle. When closed it should have the minimum clearance between the top of the padlock and the shackle.

Digital keypad locks (right)

The mechanism locks automatically when the door is closed and can be opened from the outside only by punching the correct number code.

Digital keypads are usually used only on the common entrance to a block of flats or offices.

Only people who are authorized to enter the block should know the code, and it should be changed at regular intervals.

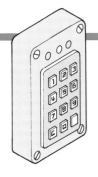

Remote control locks

This type of lock is activated by an infra-red beam from a hand-held device and is usually used only on garage doors and driveway gates.

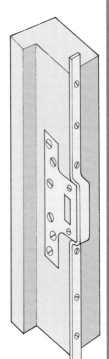

LOCKS 3

REMEMBER!
● *Locks are useless if you are careless with your keys (see pp. 28-9).*
● *Your Crime Prevention Officer can tell you which kind of locks to use.*

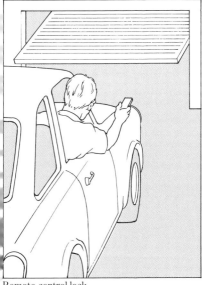

Remote control lock

STEEL REINFORCING STRIPS

You can buy metal strips to screw to the door frame to strengthen it against a jemmy attack or a bodily pressure attack on the door.

WINDOWS 1

The majority of break-ins are made through windows. In addition to providing a way in, they can give burglars a good idea of the general value of the property inside. Here are some simple ways to deter thieves.

● Hang net curtains to obscure the view during the daytime.
● Turn any electrical equipment with an illuminated face, such as a video recorder, to face away from the window.
● Close curtains or blinds at night.

FIXED WINDOWS
Because burglars break windows in order to open them rather than climb through them, fixed windows are more secure than opening ones.

However, if you want to replace any of your opening windows with fixed ones, check with your local authority first to make sure you are complying with building regulations.

CASEMENT WINDOWS
Casements are the most common type of window in modern houses. They can be hinged at the side or top, or pivot vertically or horizontally. They usually have a cockspur handle.

On small and medium-sized casements you may be able to replace the cockspur handle with

1 Key operated screw

a handle incorporating a lock. Or you can fit a locking cockspur handle stop.

On larger casements, which are vulnerable to leverage attacks, fit locks at the points shown in the illustrations opposite.

On some wooden casements you can fit mortise bolts. These are smaller than the mortise bolts for doors and fit into the window section; the bolts shoot into the frame.

There are three categories of lock and a variety of models to suit the different styles of casement and wooden, metal or aluminium frames.

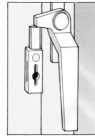

2 Locking cockspur handle

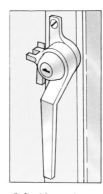

3 Locking cockspur handle stop

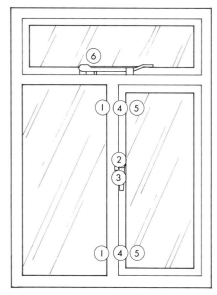

Position of locks on casement windows

● Install locks on all basement and ground floor windows, and upper storey windows that can be reached from a flat roof, mature tree or drainpipe.

Key operated
You use a key to secure and release the lock.

Keys
Many manufacturers have a single key pattern to operate all their locks, while others have a variety.
   The latter offer more security, but there are so many different window locks in existence that a burglar would have to carry bundles of keys to give him any chance of unlocking your window.

Automatic
This device locks automatically when you shut the window. You unlock it with a key.

Manually operated
You press a plunger on the side of the lock to secure it. You unlock it with a key.

FANLIGHTS
Fanlights are small top-hung casements. They are kept closed by a casement stay, which can be locked with a casement stay screw or stop. You can also secure them with casement locks.

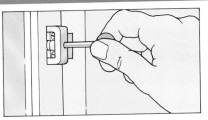

4 Key operated lock

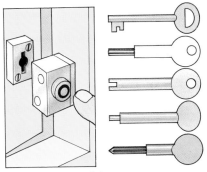

5 Manually operated plunger

6 Fanlight screw lock

REMEMBER!
● *An open window is an invitation to burglars.*
● *Upstairs windows are vulnerable if they can be reached from a nearby roof or by climbing a tree or drainpipe.*
● *Window locks are an effective deterrent and also provide physical protection.*
● *Fitting locks to many windows is a simple DIY job (see pp. 44-5).*
● *Get professional advice about fitting locks to windows with soft (aluminium or plastic) frames.*
● *Entry in more than 50% of domestic burglaries is gained through a window.*

WINDOWS 2

SASH WINDOWS
Sash windows slide up and down. The top and bottom halves may each be a single pane of glass or may be subdivided into smaller panes.

Aluminium frames
Many aluminium sashes are installed with a locking fitch catch.

If yours are not, ask your Crime Prevention Officer, a locksmith or the window manufacturer about replacing the ordinary fitch catch or adding another type of lock.

Wooden frames
Many older, wooden-framed sashes do not have locking fitch catches but they are easy to install.

You can also fit key-operated locking stops to each side of the upper sash. Position them to lock the window when it is closed, and 10 cm (4 in) from the bottom of the upper sash to lock it open for ventilation.

For narrow window stiles, use dual screws. A barrel screws into the top rail of the bottom sash, and a bolt screws into the barrel to lock the upper sash.

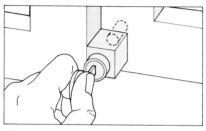
Key-operated sash lock

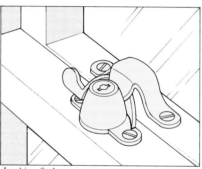
Locking fitch cap

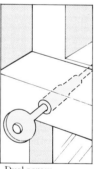

Dual screw

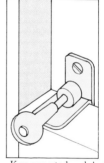
Key-operated sash lock

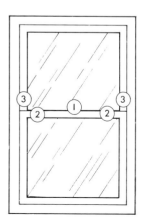

FITTING LOCKS
You can fit window locks yourself if you have reasonable DIY skills.

Be careful not to break the window pane by screwing through the frame into the part of the glass concealed there.

You need the following information about your windows when choosing suitable locks.

● Construction: wooden, metal, or plastic frames.
● Style: horizontal, vertical or side-hung casement; sash; louvre; sliding horizontal.
● Width of stile or rail on which the lock is to be fixed.

Lock placement
1 Locking fitch cap
2 Dual screw
3 Key-operated sash lock

WINDOWS 2

HORIZONTALLY SLIDING WINDOWS

You can buy locks that are smaller versions of patio door locks (see p. 43).

LOUVRE WINDOWS

Louvre windows are the most vulnerable of all opening windows because the individual blades are easy to remove.

If you don't want to replace them with more conventional windows, secure the blades in the frame with epoxy resin adhesive and install a special louvre lock.

SKYLIGHTS/ ROOFLIGHTS

These windows can be very difficult to secure properly, and you might need to install bars or a grille (see pp. 46-7). Ask your Crime Prevention Officer for advice.

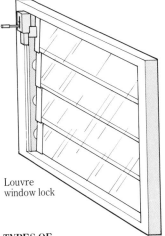

Louvre window lock

TYPES OF GLASS

Ordinary glass will shatter into sharp, jagged pieces under impact.

If there are children, or disabled or infirm people in your home who might fall against any glazed area, there are two types of safety glass you can use.

● Laminated glass offers the greatest security and safety for windows and glazed areas of external doors. It may crack, but it will not break under impact.

● Toughened or tempered glass is a safety glass for internal glazed areas.

It is four to five times stronger than ordinary glass of the same thickness. If it breaks, it shatters into small, virtually harmless pieces without any sharp edges.

You cannot cut tempered glass – it will shatter – so order the exact size you need.

● Reeded and frosted glass are variations of ordinary glass. They are not safety glass and do not offer any greater security.

REMEMBER!

● *Every window that can be opened can be locked.*

● *Some windows can be locked when they are slightly open for ventilation.*

● *Consult your local authority before installing fixed windows.*

WINDOWS 3

In most circumstances window locks provide a reasonable level of security. However, if you live in a high risk area or have very valuable property in your home, you might want to consider strengthening the defence of your windows.

GRILLES

Fixed bars
Iron bars embedded into the surrounding masonry can be installed inside or outside the window.

They might be used to protect a vulnerable lavatory window, but they are not often used for other windows.
● They are ugly.
● They make cleaning the window difficult.
● In the event of a fire in the house the window cannot be used as an emergency exit.

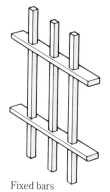

Fixed bars

Hinged grille
The grille fits on the inside of the window. It is hinged at one side and locked at the other, so it can be opened if you want to clean the window or use it as an emergency exit.

Sliding grilles
A sliding grille is similar to an old-fashioned sliding lift gate. It is useful for protecting large areas of glass, such as patio doors and balcony windows and doors.

When the house is empty, the grille can be pulled across and locked to form an internal barrier. When the house is occupied, the grille can be pulled back and hidden behind the curtains.

Detachable grilles
A detachable grille is made specifically for the window it protects.

It lifts in and out of the interior window space. In position it is secured by fixed locks or padlocks.
● It can be removed during the day when the house is occupied and replaced at night and when the house is empty.
● It does not interfere with window cleaning.
● The window can be used as an emergency exit if necessary.

Detachable grille

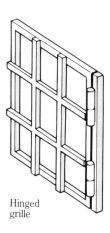

Hinged grille

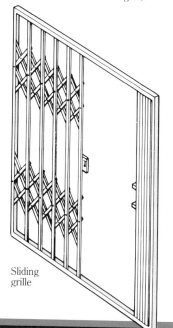

Sliding grille

WINDOWS 3

DESIGN

Except for the fixed bars and sliding grille, grilles are made in a wide range of designs.

The quality of the metal, the manufacture and the installation will determine the level of security the grille provides. Get professional advice before buying or installing a grille.

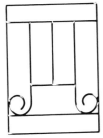

Grille designs

SHUTTERS

Solid wooden shutters are an alternative to metal grilles. Quality and correct installation are as important as for grilles, so get professional advice.

Louvred wooden shutters are decorative, but do not provide the same security as solid ones.

Solid wooden shutters

REMEMBER!

● *Keep the keys to locked grilles in a safe but convenient place so you can open them in an emergency.*

● *Your Crime Prevention Officer can advise you on the best security for your home.*

GARAGES, SHEDS and other OUTBUILDINGS

When you are making your home secure, you must remember to protect your garage, shed or other outbuildings too. In addition to your car or other vehicles, these buildings probably contain tools and equipment that not only are valuable in themselves but can also provide burglars with the help they need to break into your home.

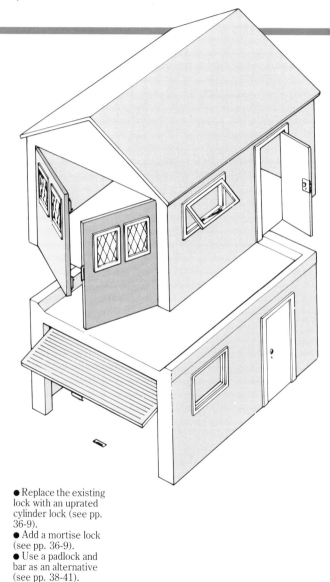

GARAGES

An integral garage is attached to the side of the house and has an internal door linking it with the home.

● If you live in a high risk area, you should treat this door in the same way as an external door (see pp. 34-41).

● On other types of garage you need locks on both the vehicle access and the personal access doors.

● If the doors are partially glazed, use deadlocks (see pp. 36-7) or fit grilles (see pp. 46-7 to prevent intruders reaching the locks or bolts.

● Fit window locks to all opening windows (see pp. 42-5).

Double-leaf doors

● Fit the locking leaf with a rim lock (see pp. 36-9).

● Fit the second leaf with one bolt at the top and another at the bottom (see pp. 38-41).

● Since the doors open outward, fit hinge bolts (see pp. 38-41).

'Up and over' doors

Metal 'up and over' doors usually come equipped with a simple ignition-type lock that burglars can easily overcome.

● Replace the existing lock with an uprated cylinder lock (see pp. 36-9).

● Add a mortise lock (see pp. 36-9).

● Use a padlock and bar as an alternative (see pp. 38-41).

HOME
SAFE

GARAGES, SHEDS and other OUTBUILDINGS

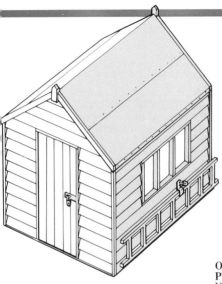

GOING OUT
Always shut and lock the garage door when you take out the car, even if you are going to be away only for a short time.

An open door to an empty garage is a clear message to burglars that no one is at home.

SHEDS
Most wooden sheds are not built to take heavy duty door locks.

Because of the general weakness of the shed, a medium duty close shackle padlock is the most cost-effective security.

Fit window locks to opening windows.

OTHER PRECAUTIONS
Never leave a ladder in your garden or at the side of your house.

A burglar will use it to get to your upstairs windows, which are probably unprotected.

If you cannot keep the ladder in the house or locked in a garage or shed, lock it to secure brackets with a chain and padlock.

Gardening tools, bricks and rubble in the garden provide burglars with ideal tools for breaking into your home. They can also be used to commit vandalism.

REMEMBER!
● *Use exterior lighting on the garage and around your building to deter burglars (see pp. 24-5).*
● *Lock your garage even if you are going out for only a few minutes.*

49

ALARMS 1

An alarm system is an electronic call for help when somebody is trying to break in, or has broken in, to your home. It should be used in addition to, not as a substitute for, good physical security.

All alarm systems have a three-stage system of operation:

1 The detectors spot intruders and signal the control.
2 The control decides whether to activate the alarm.
3 The alarm bell rings or a message is sent to the police.

It is important that everyone in the home understands how the system works, and how to switch it on and off. Otherwise there may be lots of false alarms, or the alarm might be left switched off when the house is empty.

Your alarm system should be designed specifically for your needs. For example, you might need a system that can't be accidentally triggered by your pets; or one that takes account of the fact that you regularly visit the kitchen for a snack in the middle of the night.

If you have persistent false alarms with a remote signalling system, the police will notify you that they will not respond until you have repaired or improved the system (see pp. 56-7).

There are four kinds of alarm protection:

1 External
2 Perimeter
3 Trap
4 Deliberately operated

EXTERNAL ALARMS

External alarms are used mainly for houses with a wealth of treasures to protect. They aim to detect intruders before they reach the shell of the building, or at the earliest opportunity.

The detectors are located in the grounds or on the boundary wall or fence. As a result, they are susceptible to false alarms caused by weather conditions, birds and animals.

A private security staff is usually employed to respond to the alarm initially; they will call the police only if they are sure there is an intruder.

External alarm systems are very expensive and can be properly installed only by professionals.

DETECTORS
Infra-red beam
A projector sends a beam of infra-red light, which is invisible to the naked eye, to a receiver.

Intruders passing between the projector and the receiver break the beam, and the receiver signals the alarm control.

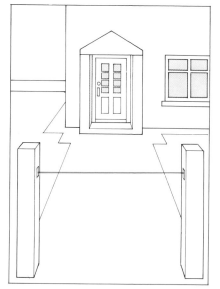

Principle of
infra-red beam

Geophone
This device monitors vibrations. It can be installed to detect activity across the ground or the vibration caused by the scaling or attacking of walls and fences.

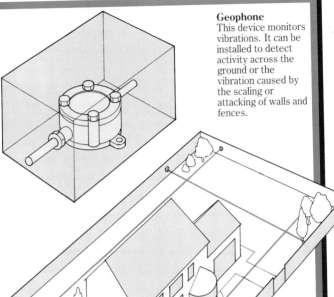

REMEMBER!

● *The bell box of an alarm system can deter burglars.*
● *An alarm system can make you feel more secure.*
● *You must maintain a good standard of psychological and physical deterrent even if you install an alarm.*

Microwave fence
A transmitter sends a pattern of invisible microwaves to a receiver.
    Intruders crossing the path between transmitter and receiver distort the pattern, and the receiver signals the alarm control.

Infra-red beams can be arranged to protect the perimeter

ALARMS 2

PERIMETER ALARMS

In this context, 'perimeter' means the shell of the building: the walls, doors and windows. The advantage of perimeter protection is that the alarm detects intruders as soon as they break in and start their burglary. This increases the likelihood of catching them, and of minimizing the damage to, and loss of, your property.

The disadvantage of these systems is that they require a great deal of wiring and

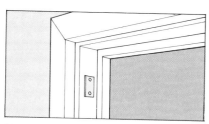

Magnetic reed contact on door frame

Infra-red beam
This is the same device as can be used to protect the exterior (see pp. 50-1).
For internal use, the beam can be projected across a doorway, window or row of windows.

DETECTORS
Magnetic reed contact
This type of switch creates an alarm when a door or window is opened.

It consists of magnetically operated reeds sealed in a small glass tube, which is enclosed in a metal or plastic case.

One contact is either surface – or flush – mounted on the door or window frame. The magnet is similarly mounted on the door or window in line with it.

The magnetic field keeps the reeds closed, allowing an electric current to flow through them.

When the door or window is opened, the magnetic field is broken. As a result, the reeds open, causing a break in the electric current and activating the alarm.

If you are using surface-mounted contacts, position them where they are least likely to be damaged by normal everyday use of the door or window.

Contacts will not work on damaged or ill-fitting doors, windows and frames.

Setting the alarm

take a lot of time to install, and so can be quite expensive in a large house. Most houses that have alarm systems use a combination of perimeter and trap alarms.

ALARMS 2

Break-glass detector

This sensor is usually used only in high risk situations. It detects the sound frequencies emitted by breaking glass.

The detector is fixed to the glass it is protecting, although some types can be put on an adjacent wall. You must be careful when cleaning the glass that you don't accidentally damage the sensor.

It is important to know what kind of glass you have in your doors or windows (see pp. 44-5). The majority of detectors will react to the sound of breaking plate glass, but not of laminated, tempered or wired glass.

Some detectors can also be set off by the sound frequencies of jangling keys or rattling bottles, causing a false alarm.

Vibration detector

This type of sensor is usually used only in situations where the value of the property is likely to attract professional burglars and when an attack is expected through the walls of the building.

The detector is placed on the walls inside the home, and picks up vibrations caused by blows or drilling. If the sensor registers the kind of vibrations that it is programmed to identify as an attack, it signals an alarm.

Pressure mat

This detector is a flat, plastic-covered contact device.

It is hidden under a carpet in front of doors and windows (see also pp. 54-5). It signals the alarm when sufficient weight is placed on it.

Although it reacts to a person walking on it, the pressure mat will also react if a large dog treads on it or you place a piece of furniture on it when it is switched on. Moving furniture on the mat can also damage the mat.

After a while the outline of the mat might become visible on the carpet, warning a burglar of its presence.

REMEMBER!

● *Ask your Crime Prevention Officer about alarm systems appropriate to your level of risk.*
● *Make sure everyone in the household knows how and when to switch the system on and off.*
● *Test your system regularly to make sure it is working properly.*

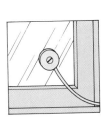

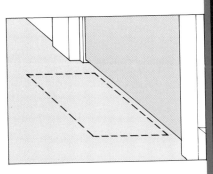

Break-glass detector   Pressure mat

ALARMS 3

TRAP ALARMS

Trap alarms are installed strategically within the home to detect intruders after they have entered. They are less expensive than perimeter systems, but allow burglars to penetrate deeper into your home.

DETECTORS
Passive infra-red detector
This movement detector is called passive because, unlike the infra-red beam, it does not transmit anything. It only receives and measures infra-red energy from other objects.

Everything with a temperature above absolute zero emits some degree of infra-red energy.

When the alarm system is switched on, the sensor adjusts to the level of infra-red energy in its field of vision. It will detect the increase in the infra-red level created by an intruder, and activate the alarm.

The sensors need to be positioned carefully. Although they are generally stable, they can react to strong sunlight or strong artificial light, warm draughts and radiated heat.

Passive infra-red detectors can be used to monitor movement in rooms or along corridors.

They can be used vertically to create an alarm curtain, for example, in front of a wall of paintings.

They can also be used to create a horizontal curtain to detect a break-in through the roof.

Passive infra-red sensor

Passive infra-red detector protecting a corridor

Passive infra-red detector protecting a room

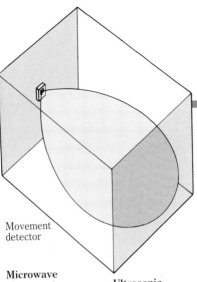

Movement
detector

Microwave movement detector

This device has a transmitter and receiver installed in a single unit.

The transmitter sends out a signal that is deflected off solid objects back to the receiver. The signal moves at a constant rate, so the return trip should take the same length of time as the outward one.

An intruder who moves into the path of the signal distorts the timing of the return signal, and this then activates the alarm.

Microwave sensors are used to detect movement in rooms, halls or corridors. They must be installed with great precision. Poor installation can result in blind spots or false alarms from external vibrations, or even from the movement of water in pipes.

Ultrasonic movement detector

This trap alarm is also based on the transmission of waves of energy. It transmits sound waves above the range audible to the human ear.

False alarms can be caused by draughts, fans, and the ringing of a telephone nearby.

Pressure mat

A pressure mat can be used as a trap alarm as well as a perimeter alarm (see pp. 52-3).

In this instance it is put under the carpet on stairs and in hallways to detect intruders moving around the house.

It can also be used to protect a particular item by placing it where a burglar would have to stand to commit the theft; for example, in front of a display cabinet.

Other trap alarms

● You can fit contact alarms (see pp. 52-3) to cabinet and cupboard doors, and to internal doors.
● There are special individual alarms for video recorders, home computers and other electrical equipment.

They can be incorporated into the main flex and will create an alarm when the wiring is cut or pulled from the wall socket, whether or not the power is on.
● Special detectors will protect individual pictures from being moved.

DELIBERATELY OPERATED ALARM

This is better known as a panic button. It is most often found in banks.

A panic button for the home can be installed just inside the front door. If you were attacked by a caller at the door, you would press the button. It would sound the alarm bell or send a message to a central alarm station, which would inform the police.

Another button could be sited in the bedroom, so you could sound the alarm if you heard intruders at night.

REMEMBER!

● *Proper installation is essential for alarm systems.*
● *Do not put furniture on top of pressure mats.*

CONTROL EQUIPMENT

You use the alarm system's control equipment to turn the alarm on and off, and to check the circuit for faults. When the system is turned on, the control equipment will activate the alarm if it receives a signal from the detectors. The alarm might be a bell only, mounted on the wall of the building, or a message sent over a telephone link to a central station, which then contacts the police.

Pre-set exit/entry
The control usually includes a time exit/entry. This feature allows you to leave and re-enter your home without setting off the alarm.
● When you are ready to go out, you switch on the alarm at the control box. You then have a set length of time in which to leave before the alarm is fully functional.
● When you return, a contact on the door starts a timer that allows you an interval in which to turn off the system. If you don't, the alarm will sound.

TYPES OF SIGNALLING

The type of signalling you choose will depend on the value of your property, the location of your home and the level of crime in the area. All systems include an interior or exterior bell, or both.

Detection zones
An alarm system can have one or more detection zones. This is how a two-zone system can be used in a small house.
● Zone one is the ground floor, protected by door and window contacts, pressure mats and a passive infra-red detector (see pp. 52-5).
● Zone two is the upstairs hall and landing, protected by a passive infra-red detector.
● When the house is empty, you turn on both zones to detect intruders breaking in on the ground floor or through an upstairs window.
● When you go to bed at night, you can switch on zone one alone, so that people can walk between the bedrooms and the bathroom without setting off the alarm.
● Deliberately operated alarms (see pp. 54-5) are always separate from an intruder detection alarm system because they remain on permanently.

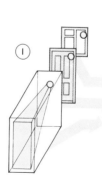

Central station

Bell only

1 Sensors detect intruder
2 Activate alarm
3 Bell rings
4 Frightens intruder
5 Sends signal by telephone
6 Operator rings police

BELL-ONLY SYSTEMS

The alarm signal can be a bell, siren or klaxon. It is located on the outside of the building, out of reach, if possible, of potential intruders.

This system provides the lowest level of protection. It relies on frightening off the burglar, and on a neighbour or passer-by notifying the police. For this reason it is not very useful in remote or isolated areas.

In systems that comply with the British Standard, the bell will sound if anyone tampers with the box.

The bell must switch itself off automatically within 20 minutes to comply with the Control of Pollution Act. It automatically re-sets itself.

REMOTE SIGNALLING SYSTEMS

These alarms sound an audible warning and send a message by telephone to a control point, from which it is relayed to the local police.

The police do not usually allow alarms to be connected directly to the station. They will respond to the relayed message only if the alarm installation conforms to BS 4737 (see pp. 60-1).

Some police forces insist that these systems have a built-in delay on the bell, so that it rings three to five minutes after the message is relayed to them. This gives them a greater chance of catching the thief.

Auto-dialler

An auto-dialler sends a recorded message to the telephone exchange on an ex-directory telephone line. The exchange then switches the recorded message through to the local police.

Although better than a bell-only system, an auto-dialler does have drawbacks .

● Most will dial 999 only once, and if the call misroutes, the police will not get the message.

● You must take care that the recorded message remains clear, otherwise the police operator might make a mistake about the address.

● The telephone line is not monitored. An alarm message might not get through if the line has been tampered with or has a fault on it.

Digital communicator

Like the auto-dialler, the digital communicator uses an ex-directory telephone line. It sends a series of coded signals to a central station run by the security company, which then notifies the police.

● It will try to pass the message several times.

● The central station signals the communicator when it has received a message.

● The telephone line is not monitored, so messages may not get through if there is a fault.

Direct private wire

This is the most secure form of signalling.

The alarm signal is transmitted on a continuously monitored private line. The central station will know immediately of any fault or interference on the line.

This is the most expensive alarm protection and is used for high risk premises.

ALARMS 4

REMEMBER!

● *About 98 per cent of all alarm calls received by the police are false.*

● *False alarms are caused by faulty equipment, weather, animals and carelessness.*

● *Police may refuse to respond to a remote-signalling alarm system.*

ALARMS 6

INSTALLATION AND MAINTENANCE

PROFESSIONAL INSTALLATION

Professionally installed alarm systems are recommended for all but very low risk situations. There is a British Standard – BS 4737 – for the installation and maintenance of alarm systems by commercial operators, but it applies only to alarms *inside* buildings. You can choose a

MAINTENANCE
BS 4737 recommends that the installing company also maintains the system. However, this is not compulsory, and you can get an independent service contract.

Preventive maintenance
To make sure that your alarm system is in good working order, it needs to be checked regularly.
BS 4737 includes inspection and test regulations for routine maintenance.
It recommends that remote signalling and battery-powered bell-only systems are checked every six months, and that bell-only systems powered by mains electricity are checked every 12 months.

Corrective maintenance
If your alarm system develops a fault, you need to have it repaired immediately.
BS 4737 requires an engineer to call within four hours of being notified of a fault in a remote signalling system.
The period may be longer for a bell-only system, but should be agreed in advance by you and the service company.
Following an alarm on a remote signalling system, most police forces insist that the alarm is reset only by an engineer. This is to prevent false alarms caused by a customer resetting a faulty system.

Maintenance records
After a maintenance visit by an engineer, you should be asked to sign a record of the visit, and be given a copy.

Stand-alone system

DIY INSTALLATION
Stand-alone system
This contains all the elements of an alarm system – detector, control and signal – in one unit.
● It detects intruders using a passive infra-red beam or ultrasonic waves (see pp. 54-5).
● Some models are powered by mains electricity, others by a rechargeable battery.
● The control includes a pre-set safe exit/entry interval (see pp. 56-7).

● The alarm signal is usually an ear-splitting siren. It is sometimes accompanied by flashing lights.
● You need a separate unit for each area you want to protect.
● Choose a robust model that will survive being hit and kicked.
● Read the instructions carefully and use the test facility.

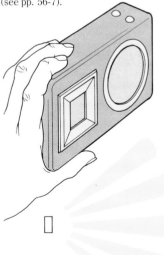

Field of detection

reputable company from the register of The National Supervisory Council for Intruder Alarms or ask your Crime Prevention Officer to recommend one.

REMEMBER!
● *Your Crime Prevention Officer can advise you on professional and DIY installations.*
● *Use professional installers who comply with BS 4737.*
● *Buy DIY kits that conform to BS 6707.*
● *Use your locks: an alarm system is not a substitute for basic security procedures.*

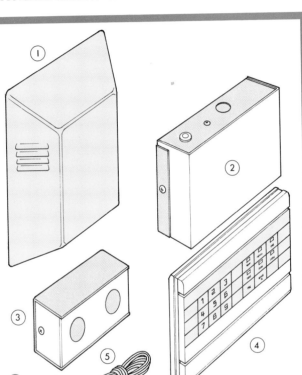

1 Bell box
2 Power supply
3 Movement detector
4 Control panel
5 Wiring
6,7 Contacts

Conventional hard wire system
This consists of individual detectors, a control box, an alarm signal and wiring.
The British Standard for DIY alarm kits – BS 6707 – provides full installation instructions and guidance on testing and maintenance.
Because house sizes vary, an alarm kit will not always provide you with the exact number and type of detectors you require. You can buy extra detectors.
● Before you buy your kit, survey your home to determine exactly what you need (see pp. 76-7).
● BS 6707-approved systems are bell-only (see pp. 56-7).

A SAFE PHILOSOPHY

A safe is an excellent last line of defence against an opportunist burglar, who is unlikely to have the time or ability to open or remove it. However, don't use a home safe to store documents, cash or jewellery that really should be deposited in a bank. Keep only essential items at home.

TYPES OF SAFE
● There is no British Standard for safes. Consult your Crime Prevention Officer or locksmith for advice on a suitable safe for your needs.

Free-standing safes
In many homes a free-standing safe is impractical because of its size or weight.
● A safe that is kept on the ground floor and weighs less than one tonne should be secured to the floor.
● A safe that is kept above ground-floor level and weighs less than 800 kg (16 cwt) should be secured to the floor.

Wall safes
A wall safe is set into the wall and replaces existing bricks. The protection it offers is determined by the quality of the safe, the standard of its installation, and its location.

● The size of a wall safe is measured by the number of bricks it replaces; you can buy a safe that is, for example, one, two or three bricks high. Most safes are one brick deep, but you can get double-depth models.
● It is best to have a wall safe installed professionally unless you are very able at DIY. It can be installed only in a brick wall.
● If the safe is set into a cavity brick wall, make sure the back of it doesn't touch the outer wall, or it can create a bridge for damp.
● If you are planning to put the safe in a party wall, make sure the wall is more than one brick deep, or you will make a hole in your neighbour's wall.
● Try to put the safe somewhere a burglar is unlikely to find it – every thief will look behind pictures. Your Crime Prevention Officer can give you some good ideas.

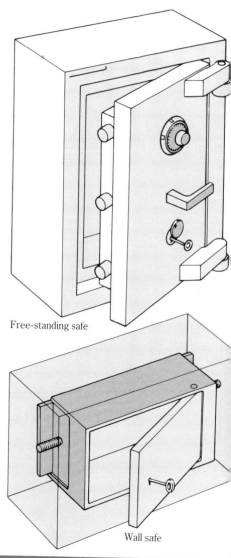

Free-standing safe

Wall safe

A SAFE PHILOSOPHY

Floor safes
These safes are recessed into the floor so that the lid is just below or at floor level. They are available in different sizes, according to the depth available under the floor, but the opening is usually relatively small.

● A floor safe is less convenient to use than other safes, since you must kneel down to open and extend your arm into it. Also, items have to be stacked vertically.

● A floor safe should be installed professionally.

● The best location is in a concrete or stone floor, but a safe can be adequately secured to the joists under wooden floorboards.

● Choose a position near the wall so that you can cover the safe with the carpet or lino, and get to it with the minimum of inconvenience.

● A floor safe is generally more secure than a wall safe since it is more difficult to lever out of place.

KEYS AND COMBINATION
● If you have a keylock safe, always take the keys with you when you leave the house.

● If you have a combination-lock safe, do not leave the combination written down anywhere in the house, and certainly not on the safe itself.

STRONG ROOMS
It is very expensive to design and build a strong room. The cost is not justified unless your property is so valuable that there is a high risk of attracting a professional, rather than opportunist, burglar.

REMEMBER!
● *A safe is a last line of defence: your main objective is to deter a burglar from approaching your property.*

● *Conceal a safe in a place where a burglar is unlikely to look for it.*

● *Keep only essential valuables at home.*

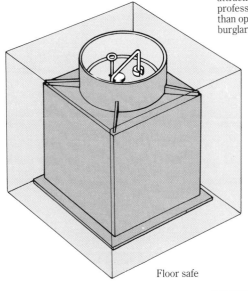

Floor safe

PROPERTY MARKING

Marking your property and displaying a 'marked property' window sticker is an easy and efficient way to deter burglars. And if your property is stolen, you have a better chance of it being recovered.

All property that is recovered by, or handed in to, the police is checked for visible marks, and is scanned with an ultraviolet lamp for invisible marks. Any mark is decoded and the owner contacted.

CODING
Every house and flat in the United Kingdom has a post code. It identifies a group of about 20 houses in a street. If you add your house number, you have a unique code that identifies the property as belonging to your home: KT8 9TD/35.

If your house has a name rather than a number, just add the first two letters of the name to your post code: KT8 9TD/WH.

MARKING
You can mark property with a permanent and visible mark, or an invisible mark that must be renewed occasionally.

Permanent and visible
Use permanent marking wherever possible, on items that it will not damage or devalue.
● It is a strong deterrent because a thief can see that the property will be difficult to sell.
● There is no chance that the mark will wear off.
● Use hammer and dies to mark only large metal objects, such as lawnmowers, garden furniture, and some bicycles (see pp. 90-1).

Aluminium is a soft metal and should not be marked in this way.
● Use a power-driven engraving tool or a hard-tipped scriber to mark items such as video recorders, televisions and microwave ovens.

Hard-tipped scriber

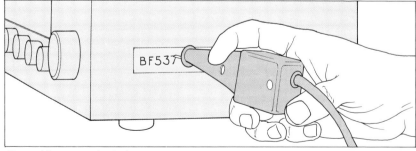

Power-driven engraving tool

PROPERTY MARKING

Invisible marking
- Apply invisible marking with an ultraviolet pen or fluid. It is invisible to the naked eye, but shows up clearly under an ultraviolet light.
- Use it on china, porcelain, silver, glass and other delicate items that would be damaged or devalued by permanent marking.
- Consult an expert before marking valuable antiques in any way.
- Check the marking under an ultraviolet light about every nine months, and renew it if it has faded or worn.

CHANGE OF ADDRESS
You can update your property marking if you move.
- Place an X after the original mark, and then add your new code under or next to it.
- Do not try to remove or obliterate the original mark.

OTHER MEANS OF IDENTIFICATION
Use the following ways of identifying your property in addition to the property marking methods described above.

Serial numbers
Some objects have serial numbers stamped on them. Make a list of all serial numbers, and keep it in a safe place.

Photographs
Photographs can be useful in identifying stolen property.
- Keep photographs of all your valuable possessions.
- Photograph objects against a plain background.
- Photograph objects front and back.
- Photograph small objects next to a ruler.
- Label each object on the back of the photograph.

REMEMBER!
- *Get permission to mark rented equipment, such as televisions and videos.*
- *Display 'marked property' stickers prominently.*
- *Update your list of serial numbers and your photographic record regularly.*
- *Check and renew your invisible marking about every nine months.*
- *Keep a detailed written list of all your valuables.*

IF the WORST HAPPENS

Arriving home to find signs that someone has entered your house or flat can be a frightening experience. For your own safety, and to help the police investigating the crime, it is important to know what to do and what not to do.

DOs AND DON'Ts

When the burglar is in your home

An open front door is a sign that the burglar might still be in your home. In that event, or if you have used your key to get in and see signs of a disturbance, and think an intruder might still be there:

● Don't go in. There could be more than one intruder, and you could be injured as they try to make their escape.

● Don't let the thief know that you have returned: leave quickly and quietly.

● Do go to a neighbour or the nearest telephone box and dial 999 to call the police.

● Do watch your home from a safe vantage point.

● If you see the burglar leave, try to get a good description of him, including his height, build, hair style and colour, whether he has any facial hair, and the type and colour of his clothing.

● Do watch which way the thief goes. If he gets in a vehicle, write down its registration number, make and colour.

● Don't try to stop him unless you are very sure that you, perhaps with your neighbour's help, do not run any risk of being hurt.

When the burglar has left

If you are sure that no one is in the house:

● Try to remain calm.

● Telephone the police immediately.

● If you are alone, ask a friend or neighbour to stay with you.

● Don't touch anything or try to put things back in place. You may destroy valuable forensic evidence in the process.

● Do try to assess what is missing while you wait for the police.

● Do try to find out how and where the burglar broke in.

WHEN THE POLICE ARRIVE

A uniformed officer will ask you for basic details:

● When you discovered the crime.

● Who you think might have committed the crime.

● The description of anyone you saw leaving the house.

● Whether you had any suspicious callers or noticed anyone suspicious in the neighbourhood recently.

● Where the burglar broke in.

● What is missing. He will ask you to provide a full list of the property that has been stolen after you have had time to check through all your belongings thoroughly.

The officer will tell you what you can touch and put away. He might put some items aside for further examination.

Depending on the clues found at the burglary, an officer from the CID (Criminal Investigation Department) might visit you subsequently.

IMMEDIATE ACTION

● Arrange for immediate repairs to broken window, locks or doors; many security companies are open 24 hours a day.

● Make sure you improve your security too: don't be burgled again.

Reporting the losses

● Immediately report the loss of savings passbooks, chequebooks, credit cards, and vehicle registration and other important documents to the relevant authorities.

● Notify the insurance company that you have been burgled, and get a claim form.

● Make a list of the missing items. If you have an inventory (see pp. 62-3, 72-5), you can check against that.

If not, try to go through your home systematically; it may take you several days or even longer to realize what is missing.

● Indicate which property can be identified by serial numbers or security code markings (see pp. 62-3).

● State the monetary value of each missing item. This will be easier if you already have an inventory.

● Locate valuations or receipts for missing items.

● Send copies of the list to the police and the insurance company, and keep a copy for yourself.

YOU THE VICTIM

Being the victim of a burglary is a very distressing experience. Studies by the Centre for Criminological Research at Oxford University have shown that, in the short term, a small percentage of victims of burglaries, particularly women, have acute reactions, including vomiting or hysteria.

A much larger percentage suffer from shivering and shaking, insomnia and a dazed or detached feeling that can last for weeks and may require medical treatment.

Most victims of burglary agree that the loss of material possessions – even those of great sentimental value – is of secondary importance. By far the worst part of a burglary is the feeling that their privacy has been invaded, emphasized by the chaos caused by the thief ransacking the home.

The reaction is similar to that of rape victims; the distress of personal violation. Some people feel that their home has become polluted, and others fear that the attack will be repeated – despite police statistics that this is most unusual.

How you'll feel
As a burglary victim, you can expect to experience a flood of emotions. It is very common to feel:
● Why me? What did I do to deserve this?
● Angry at the unseen intruder.
● Angry at society in general.
● Angry at yourself or someone else for poor security.
● Distressed at the loss of irreplaceable possessions.
● Irritated at the inconvenience.
● Disgusted at the mess.
● Frustrated because there is nothing you can do to recover your goods.
● Annoyed because the police may seem to treat the crime as matter-of-fact.

● Frightened of the burglar because you did not see him.
● Apprehensive that you'll be burgled again.
● Overwhelming revulsion at the invasion of your privacy, and a need to clean everything.

How to cope
● Try to understand and express your feelings.
● Discuss the experience with your family or friends. Ask for their help and support.
● Talk to your doctor, clergyman or other counsellor.
● Get in touch with your local Victims Support Scheme (see pp. 150-1) for practical help and moral support.

Be prepared
Think about the effects a burglary might have on you. A mental rehearsal need not be a pessimistic exercise; it could help you act more sensibly in the event.

More importantly, it could motivate you to take steps NOW to maximize your home security so that the worst never happens.

IF the WORST HAPPENS

REMEMBER!
● *Good home security minimizes your risk of being a victim of burglary.*
● *Don't confront a burglar in your home.*
● *If you are burgled ring 999 for the police.*
● *Don't touch anything until the police have arrived.*
● *Get help and advice from family, friends, and your local Victims Support Scheme.*

FIRE! 1

FIRE PREVENTION

An accidental fire in your home shares two important characteristics with the crimes described in this book.

1 It can result in loss of property and in harm to yourself or your family.
2 It can usually be prevented.

Most household fires start when a normally harmless use of fire – a cooker, a

---

General precautions
● Keep halls and stairs clear of obstacles and fire hazards.
● Keep doors to communal staircases closed.
● Don't use a candle or other naked flame for lighting, especially in a bedroom, workshop or loft.
● Never hang washing over gas, electric or paraffin heaters or fires.
● Make sure portable heaters are stable and kept where they will not be knocked over.
● Don't use or keep petrol in the home.
● Store flammable liquids in a cool place, in strong, small, clearly labelled screw-top containers away from the heat.
● Keep butane gas lighter fuel and aerosol cans away from heat. Don't burn or puncture empty containers.

● Use non-combustible materials for loft insulation.
● Use only flame-retardent nightwear and bedding.
● Make sure upholstered furniture conforms to safety standards; polyurethane foam is lethal when ignited.
● Throw out old newspapers and cleaning rags that have been used with flammable solvents.
● Use only safety matches.
● Keep toys and papers away from direct heat.

Before going to bed
● Switch off and unplug all electric appliances not in use.
● Turn off gas appliances.
● Ensure open fires are damped and guarded.
● Check that there are no smouldering cigarettes in any room.
● Close all internal doors to slow or contain a fire if one should start.

In the kitchen
● Avoid using expanded polystyrene tiles on the ceiling. If they are already there, do not decorate them with an oil-based paint.
● Never fill deep fat fryers more than half full. Make sure that the foods you are about to fry have a dry surface to avoid spitting.
   Always switch off the heat if you leave the pan, even for a moment.
   A covered automatic deep fat fryer is the safest.
● Don't hang dish towels anywhere on the cooker or on the oven door.
● Don't lean over the hob when the burner is on.

Electrical appliances
● Switch off and unplug appliances not in use.
● Install enough electric sockets to avoid long trailing wires and multiple-plug adaptors.
● Keep flexes away from naked flames and hot surfaces.
● Replace worn or damaged flexes immediately.
● Use purpose made connectors to join flex; never twist the wires together.
● During a power failure, switch off all appliances that might come on again if power is restored while you are asleep or out of the house.
● Never run an appliance from a light bulb socket.
● Never cover a light bulb with paper or fabric.
● Use earthed three-pin plugs with the correct fuses. Keep a stock of fuses and fuse wire, and make sure you know the wiring colours.

heater, a cigarette – gets out of control through neglect or abuse. Kitchen fires are the most common, but most fire deaths are a result of fires that start in bedrooms and living rooms.

FIRE! 1

- Don't use time switches or thermo-stats on radiant coil or bar fires.
- Don't use electric underblankets as overblankets, or the reverse. Keep blankets dry and uncreased, and have them serviced every three years.
  Discard electric blankets that do not have a BS3456 label.

Gas appliances

- Keep rooms where gas appliances are used well ventilated.
- Check that pilot lights and ignition devices are working properly.
- Make sure disused gas points are properly plugged and capped; consult your local gas board for advice.
- Fit all gas heaters with a fire guard.
- Always be ready to light burners *before* you turn on the gas.

Bottled gas

- Change cylinders outdoors or in a thoroughly ventilated room.
- Store spare cylinders in a frost-free outbuilding and well away from heat. Don't keep more than you need.
- Make sure both taps are off before changing cylinders.
- Always replace the safety cap on the valve when a cylinder is empty or not in use.
- Never remove the regulator or adaptor on a self-sealing connector while the heater is on.
- Test for a suspected leak by brushing soapy water over the joint. If bubbles appear, put on the cap and leave the cylinder outdoors until it can be checked by an engineer.
  Never test by using a match.

Solid-fuel fires

- Use a fire guard in front of the fireplace.
- Have the chimney swept at least once a year.
- Keep a metal container by the fireside for removing ashes.
- Never use petrol or paraffin to start the fire.
- Don't draw the fire by holding a sheet of paper in front of it.
- Always damp down the fire before going out or to bed.
- If you suspect a chimney fire, call the fire brigade immediately and clear away anything that might catch fire, such as the hearth rug.

Smokers

- Extinguish all smoking materials completely as soon as you have finished with them.
- Never leave a lit cigarette, cigar or pipe on the edge of an ashtray or where it could fall onto furniture or the carpet.
- Never empty ashes into wastepaper baskets.
- Never smoke in bed or when you are sleepy.

REMEMBER!

If you smell gas:
- *Extinguish all cigarettes, flames and potential ignition sources.*
- *Open doors and windows.*
- *Check that no pilot lights have gone out or unlit taps were left on: if not, you probably have a leak.*
- *Turn off the supply at the meter.*
- *Ring the gas authority emergency telephone number immediately and report a leak.*
- *Never try to repair a gas leak yourself.*

- *Most fire fatalities occur at night.*
- *Children and the elderly are at an increased risk; they are less able to save themselves without help.*
- *Never leave children under 12 alone in the home.*
- *Keep matches and lighters away from children.*

FIRE! 2

DETECTING AND EXTINGUISHING

Even if you are careful and take all the recommended precautions, it is still possible for a fire to start accidentally.

Time is of the essence in detecting a fire to minimize the danger to people and damage to property.

Most fire fatalities occur at night because a sleeping household is much

---

DETECTORS
Heat-sensitive detectors can be used in the kitchen.

Smoke-sensitive detectors are suitable for every room except the kitchen. There are two types.
● The photo-electric detector sounds a warning when its light beam is disturbed.
● The ionization detector sounds a warning when it detects excess carbon particles in the air.

Domestic fire detectors are compact, self-contained, moderately priced and easy to install. They come with batteries and many include a test facility.

Installation
Single station units work independently of each other.

Interconnected units all sound the alarm when any one of them is activated. Most detectors can be interconnected so you can add units over a period of time.

Smoke detectors can also be hooked up to a household burglar alarm.

Ideally, install a detector in every room. If that is not possible, put one unit in the downstairs hall

and one in the upstairs landing of a house, or one centrally located in a flat.
● Position detectors on the ceiling or one the wall about 30 cm (12 in) from the ceiling.
● Don't put detectors where air conditioning

or heat ducts could deflect smoke.
● Check to see that the alarm is loud enough to wake you in your bedroom when you are sleeping with the door shut.
● Install detectors in the rooms of elderly people and smokers.

● Replace batteries and clean the units once a year.
● Test the sensing device and alarm monthly, and when you return home after a holiday or weekend break.

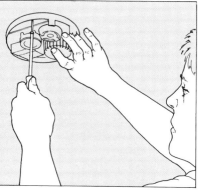

Positioning a smoke detector

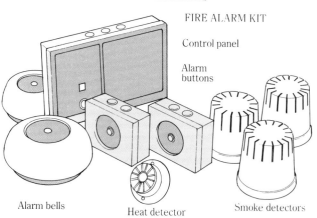

FIRE ALARM KIT

Control panel

Alarm buttons

Alarm bells

Heat detector

Smoke detectors

slower at detecting a fire. Even a fire starting in the day in an unoccupied room can go unnoticed. Fire detectors help to overcome this problem.

FIRE SAFETY EQUIPMENT

Fire extinguishers larger than the minimum recommended size (MRS) should still be small enough to handle. Choose a controllable discharge model.

Mount the extinguisher on a wall where it is visible and accessible.

Use the correct type of extinguisher.
● Water: any fire except those involving electrical equipment or inflammable liquids. Water is ideal for putting out paraffin (oil convector) heater fires where the paraffin is sealed in.
   MRS: 4.5 l (1 gal)
● Dry powder: fires involving electrical equipment and inflammable liquids *except* oil.
   MRS: 1 kg (2.2 lb)
● Carbon dioxide: burning wood, paper or textiles.
   MRS: 1 kg (2.2 lb)
● Halon: any household fire, except smouldering fires (see also pp. 94-5).
   MRS: 750 g (1.6 lb)
● Fire blanket: useful for fat fires in the kitchen. It smothers a small fire's oxygen supply. Hold it in front of you as a shield, then drop it over the fire.

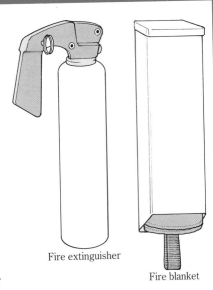

Fire extinguisher

Fire blanket

Using a fire blanket to extinguish a fire

REMEMBER!
● *Read the operating instructions for the fire extinguisher* now *so you will know what to do in an emergency.*
● *Home safety equipment can help tackle a small fire, but only the fire brigade can handle a big blaze. Never put yourself, your family or your home at risk by trying to do it yourself.*
● *Never try to put out a chip pan fire with water.*

69

FIRE! 3

ESCAPE

Make sure all the members of your household know what to do if there is a fire. Knowing the right procedures in advance will save time and could save lives.

FIRE DRILL
● Plan escape routes, preferably through the front door, from every room in your home. Vary them according to the location of the fire.
● Never use a lift in the event of fire.
1 Keep a torch handy – fires often cause electrical blackouts.
● Make sure everyone knows how to unlock the front door. Keep the key handy.
2 Plan how to help very young, very old, infirm or disabled members of the family.

WHEN FIRE STRIKES
If you cannot extinguish it quickly and safely
● Yell FIRE! to raise the alarm.
3 Get everyone out of the house, closing internal doors behind you as you go.
4 If there is a lot of smoke, crawl along the floor, where the air is clearer.
5 Dial 999 from the nearest telephone and ask for the fire brigade.
● If your home adjoins others, evacuate the neighbours.

If you are trapped in a room
6 Close the door and fanlight, and block up any gaps around them with clothing or bedding.
7 Lean out of the window to get fresh air and to shout for help. If the smoke is worse out there, close the window and lie on the floor and wait for the fire brigade.
8 If conditions are so bad that you must escape before the fire brigade arrives, make a rope by knotting sheets together. Tie one end to the bed or other heavy piece of furniture and lower yourself out of the window.
9 If you can't make a rope, drop mattresses or cushions out of the window first to break your fall.

Go out of the window feet first and lower yourself to the full extent of your arms before you drop.

If the room is more than one floor up, don't drop unless there is absolutely no choice.
10 If the window won't open, smash the glass with a chair or other heavy object.

Clear the jagged pieces from the lower edge and cover it with a heavy coat or blanket to protect yourself from injury while escaping.

FIRE! 3

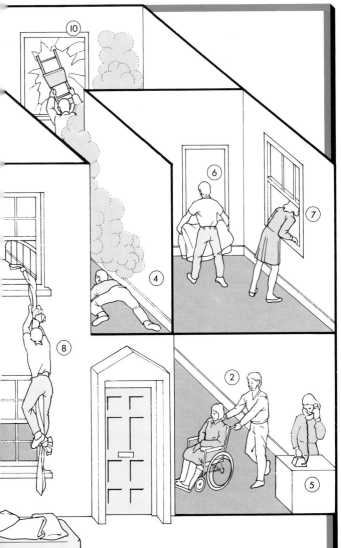

REMEMBER!
● *Never re-enter a house where there has been a fire until the fire brigade gives permission.*
● *Never use a lift in a building where there is a fire.*

INSURANCE 1

Even if you minimize your chances of being the victim of a burglary or fire it is still wise to insure your property against these, and other damage or loss. Although you may think that individually none of your possessions is valuable, it can be very expensive to have to replace all of them at once – for example, after a fire. Keep a copy of your inventory somewhere outside the home for just such an eventuality.

Household insurance is divided into three main categories: buildings, contents

BUILDINGS

Coverage

This insurance covers the cost of repairing or rebuilding the fabric, or structure, of the house or flat if it is damaged or destroyed by intruders, fire, flood, or other specified perils. The fabric of the building includes the foundations, walls and roof, and the doors, windows, floors and ceilings.

Buildings cover also incorporates permanent fixtures and fittings, such as central heating, bathtubs and sinks; and permanent external fixtures and fittings such as outbuildings, balconies, swimming pools, footpaths, fences and gates.

Premiums

Premiums for home buildings are calculated on the basis of the sum insured, and on other factors, such as construction and location. Thus a timber-framed or thatch-roofed house, or a house or block of flats in a high-crime inner-city area might attract a higher premium than a stone building with a tiled roof in a quiet suburb.

Valuation

Some insurance companies ask you to calculate the amount for which the building is to be insured, based on the cost of rebuilding it in the same materials at current prices. Others calculate the amount for you. The maximum payable on a Buildings claim is the index-linked (see opposite) rebuilding cost, which is *not* the same as the market value.

Get professional advice if you are calculating the amount to be insured. If your estimate is too low, the settlement of any claim will be reduced in proportion to the amount you were under-insured. If your estimate is too high, you will receive only the amount of compensation necessary to repair or replace your property, even though you have paid a higher premium.

CONTENTS

Coverage

Contents insurance reimburses you for certain damage to, or loss of, all household items and personal property that usually remain in the home, including clothing, furniture, appliances and ornaments.

Insurance companies label the burglar's favourite targets, such as televisions, hi-fi equipment, video recorders, home computers and microwave ovens, as 'high risk' items. They usually limit the amount of compensation they will pay for any one article, set or collection to a specific sum or to a percentage of the total amount for which you are insured. Make sure that these limits are adequate. If they are not, you can get 'all risks' coverage for specific items.

Premiums

You can choose a policy in which the premium is based on your estimate of the full cost of replacing your property at current prices. This new-for-old coverage does not apply to clothing or bedlinens, for which depreciation is taken into account.

Alternatively, you may choose a policy in which the premium is based on the original cost of the property. In the event of a claim, the insurers would pay you what the property was worth after taking wear and

and specified items and/or personal possessions covered away from home. The items covered in each category may vary from policy to policy. Read all the small print and be sure of your coverage before you agree to any policy.

tear into consideration. This used-value coverage is less expensive, but any compensation may not be enough to repair or replace your property.

Valuation
Use the checklists on pages 74-5 to help you estimate the value of your property.

'ALL RISKS'

Coverage
This policy insures items you wear or use away from home, such as jewellery, furs, cameras and sports equipment; and specified individual items of high value, such as works of art and antiques. There are five categories of 'all risks' insurance.

● Unspecified valuables: those objects individually worth less than one set figure (say £500) and collectively worth less than another set figure (say £5,000).

● Clothing: including furs and other particularly valuable garments.

● Named items: the higher-value pieces of jewellery, musical instruments, works of art, ornaments, stamp and coin collections. A professional valuation and sometimes a photograph of each item is required.

It is your responsibility to keep the insured sums up to date, since appreciation is not taken into account.

● Sports equipment.

● Money and credit card loss liability.

Premiums
Premiums and claims are based on the amounts insured; there is no new-for-old protection and no depreciation allowance.

INDEX LINKING
Most policies are index-linked so that the sums insured under 'buildings' and 'contents' are automatically up-dated every month within the period insured, at no extra premium.

Buildings insurance is linked to the House Rebuilding Cost Index issued by the Royal Institution of Chartered Surveyors.

Contents insurance is linked to the Durable Goods Section of the Retail Price Index.

Insurers offer this inflation protection on the understanding that the original sums insured are accurate.

EXCLUSIONS
Always check your policy to see what it *doesn't* cover. For example, documents such as deeds, securities, bonds and manuscripts usually must be insured separately.

Most policies also exclude coverage if your home is unoccupied for more than 30 consecutive days – an important point if you are planning a longer holiday or business trip.

INSURANCE 1

REMEMBER!
Insurance companies may offer reduced premiums if you:
● *Have an alarm system;*
● *Maintain a high standard of security, even without an alarm system;*
● *Are a member of a Neighbourhood Watch scheme;*
● *Have specified fire detection and fire-fighting equipment;*
● *Are a non-smoking household.*

Also remember:
● *Read your policy carefully. It is a legal contract.*
● *It is your responsibility to up-date your insurance, for example if you make any home improvements or acquire any new possessions.*

INSURANCE 2

MAKING AN INVENTORY

Use the checklists below to help you determine the amount of Contents insurance you need. Go through your home one room at a time and estimate the cost of replacing each item at its current price in the shops.

Remember to include any rented items, such as televisions and videos. Total the

Living room and study

£......Carpets
£......Curtains
£......Sofa
£......Chairs
£......Footstool
£......Coffee table
£......Occasional tables
£......Desk
£......Lamps and lighting fixtures
£......Shelves
£......Cabinets
£......Storage units
£......Books
£......Ornaments
£......Clocks
£......Mirrors
£......Television
£......Video recorder
£......Radio
£......Stereo/hi-fi equipment
£......Tapes and records
£......Computer hardware
£......Computer software
£......Typewriter
£......Documents
£......Portable heaters
£......Plants and containers
£......Musical instruments
£......Photograph albums
£......Miscellaneous

£......SUBTOTAL

Dining room

£......Carpets
£......Curtains
£......Lamps and lighting fixtures
£......Table
£......Chairs
£......Sideboard/bar
£......China
£......Glass
£......Cutlery
£......Table linen
£......Table mats
£......Pictures
£......Ornaments
£......Clocks
£......Mirrors
£......Portable heaters
£......Plants and containers
£......Miscellaneous

£......SUBTOTAL

Kitchen

£......Floor covering
£......Curtains or blinds
£......Table
£......Chairs and stools
£......Lighting fixtures
£......Cooker
£......Microwave oven
£......Refrigerator
£......Freezer
£......Dishwasher
£......Washing machine
£......Dryer
£......Small appliances
£......Crockery
£......Cooking utensils
£......Storage jars
£......Food
£......Drink
£......Miscellaneous

£......SUBTOTAL

Bathroom

£......Carpet
£......Curtains or blinds
£......Toiletries
£......Scales
£......Towels
£......Linen basket
£......Beauty/hygiene appliances (hair dryer, razor, etc.)
£......Lighting fixtures
£......Chair
£......Plants and containers
£......Miscellaneous

£......SUBTOTAL

Hall, stairs and landing

£......Carpet
£......Table
£......Chairs
£......Pictures
£......Ornaments
£......Lamps and lighting fixtures
£......Plants and containers
£......Miscellaneous

£......SUBTOTAL

Bedroom 1

£......Carpet
£......Curtains
£......Bed
£......Bedding
£......Wardrobe
£......Chest of drawers
£......Dressing table
£......Chairs
£......Bedside tables
£......Lamps and lighting fixtures
£......Pictures
£......Ornaments
£......Clock
£......Mirrors
£......Clothing
£......Appliances (radio, TV, tea-maker, etc.
£......Portable heaters
£......Plants and containers
£......Toys and games
£......Arts and crafts work
£......Musical instruments
£......Cameras and film
£......Needlework
£......Sports equipment
£......Miscellaneous

£......SUBTOTAL

amount for each room or area separately, and then add them all together to obtain the grand total.

INSURANCE 2

Bedroom 2

£......Carpet
£......Curtains
£......Bed
£......Bedding
£......Wardrobe
£......Chest of drawers
£......Dressing table
£......Chairs
£......Bedside tables
£......Lamps and lighting fixtures
£......Pictures
£......Ornaments
£......Clock
£......Mirrors
£......Clothing
£......Appliances (radio, TV, tea-maker, etc.)
£......Portable heaters
£......Plants and containers
£......Toys and games
£......Arts and crafts work
£......Musical instruments
£......Cameras and film
£......Needlework
£......Sports equipment
£......Miscellaneous

£......SUBTOTAL

Garage, workshop and storeroom

£......Car accessories (roofrack, tool kit, etc.)
£......Decorating equipment and supplies
£......Garden furniture
£......Work bench and tools
£......Garden tools (lawnmower, hose, rake, spade, etc.)
£......Camping equipment
£......Vacuum cleaner
£......Luggage
£......Sewing machine
£......Miscellaneous

£......SUBTOTAL

£...............GRAND TOTAL

MAKING A CLAIM

● Get a claim form from the insurance company.
● Make a complete list of every item lost, damaged or destroyed, and its value.
● Locate the relevant receipts, bills or professional valuations.
● After receipt of your claim, the insurance company may send a loss adjuster to recommend a figure for settlement.
● If you are not happy with the insurer's estimate, you can hire a public loss assessor. For large claims, he will charge a percentage of the claim, plus VAT. You must pay his costs; they cannot form part of the claim.
● If your insurer is a member of the Ombudsman Scheme you can refer the claim to the Insurance Ombudsman free of charge.
● If your home is temporarily uninhabitable, your policy might allow you to claim expenses for alternative accommodation while it is being repaired, provided the work is begun without delay.

REMEMBER!

● *Your insurance may be void if your loss is a result of negligence – for example if you leave a window open, a door unlocked, or a key outside.*
● *Some insurers state that the insured person must take all reasonable precautions to protect his or her property.*
● *When you renew your policy after a large claim, your insurers may insist you take specific additional security measures.*
● *Some insurers offer automatic extra Contents cover for the Christmas season and the period around a wedding.*
● *No insurance policy can make up for the sentimental or personal value of some losses; insurance is no substitute for proper home security.*

TARGET HARDENING

There is a vast variety of hardware that you can use to protect your property against an intruder who does get past the perimeter barrier. This kind of security is called target hardening. It should make the thief realize that he faces an enormous task if he tries to break into your house, and it should stop him if he does try.

There are three ways to decide the best method of target hardening your home.

Private survey
The job of a representative of a private security company is to sell that company's goods and services.

A reputable firm will send a representative who has been properly trained and is competent. He will:
● Accurately assess the risk potential of your house or flat.
●Advise on the correct hardware you need to protect your home from a successful attack.
● Give details of competent installers (in most cases, his own company).
● Charge a reasonable fee.

A representative who is not honest or competent might:
● Wrongly assess the risk potential of your home.
● Leave loopholes that a burglar can exploit.
● Recommend more equipment than is necessary.
● Recommend installers who are incapable of fitting security equipment.
● Charge an unreasonably high fee.

Police survey
The Crime Prevention Officer is an experienced police officer who:
● Has had an intensive training in crime prevention.
● Is employed solely on crime prevention duties.
● Is totally impartial about products, suppliers and installers.
● Knows the current crime situation and possible future trends in your area.
● Is at your service free of charge.

Your own survey
Use the information in this chapter and the checklists on these pages to assess your risk and improve the security of your home.

You can still get advice from your Crime Prevention Officer about crime trends to help you assess the risks.

If you are a reasonably able DIY person, you should also be able to implement most of the work yourself.

DO YOUR OWN SURVEY

RISK ASSESSMENT
Answer the questions below to determine your risk level and the type of security you need:

Neighbourhood
Do you live in a:
– high risk area?
– medium risk area?
– low risk area?
If you're not sure, ask your Crime Prevention Officer or insurance company.

Type of home
(see pp. 14-17)
Do you live in a:
– detached house?
– semi-detached house?
– terraced house?

Do you live in a flat:
– on the ground floor in a purpose-built block?
– on an upper storey in a purpose-built block?
– in the basement or on the ground floor in a conversion?
– on an upper storey in a conversion?

Points of entry
Is your home accessible from the:
– front only?
– front and side(s)?
– front and back?
– front, side(s) and back?

Can you enter your home through:
– a front door?
– a side door?
– a back door?
– patio doors?
– french windows?
– ground floor windows?
– upper storey windows accessible by climbing?
– skylight?
– cellar door?
– attached garage?

SECURITY CHECKLISTS
1 Put an X by all the questions to which you can answer 'yes'.
2 Put a tick by any relevant security measures you still need to take to protect your home.

Re-read the information on the pages indicated and follow the advice given there.
3 Cross your ticks when you have carried out each measure.

Natural surveillance
(see pp. 20-1)
– Can the doors and windows to your home be seen clearly by passers-by or neighbours?
– Is the upper half of the enclosed porch glazed?

- Get a survey from a private security company.
- Get a survey from the local police Crime Prevention Officer.
- Produce your own survey.

TARGET HARDENING

REMEMBER!

The best way to defeat a burglar is to remove the target property from his grasp.

Assess the monetary and sentimental value of the property in your home, and consider the problems it might cause you if it were lost or destroyed.

If you decide that you have any of the following kinds of property that you do not need to keep at home, remove it to a secure place such as a bank.

- *Excess cash.*
- *Jewellery.*
- *Documents such as wills, deeds, bonds or legal contracts.*
- *Porcelain, paintings, stamp or coin collections.*

Perimeter barriers
(see pp. 22-3)
Does your property have a wall, fence or railings:
– at the front and sides?
– at the sides and back?
– all around?

Is your gate:
– solid/unclimbable?
– fitted with locks or bolts?

Deterrents
Do you display:
– an alarm box?
– a Beware the Dog sign?
– Neighbourhood Watch and marked property stickers (see pp. 62-3)?

– Are your drainpipes unclimbable (see pp. 24-5)?

Lighting
(see pp. 26-7)
Does your house have exterior lighting:
– above all doors?
– on the front wall?
– on the garage?
– on the drive/path?

Access control
(see pp. 28-33)
– Are all your spare keys kept in a safe place?

Does your front door have a:
– door viewer?
– chain or limiter?
– audio or audio-visual entry system?

External doors
(see pp. 34-5)
– Are all doors of recommended construction?
– Are weak doors reinforced?
– Are glazed doors and panels protected by a grille?
– Are all doors and frames in good condition?
– Is the letterbox more than 40 cm (15¾ in) from the lock?

Locks
(see pp. 36-41)
Do all external house doors have:
– a deadlock?
– hinge bolts?
– mortise or surface bolts?
– Are external cellar flaps secured inside with a padlock and hasp?

Windows
(see pp. 42-7)
– Are all window frames in good condition?
– Do all windows have locks?
– Are all especially vulnerable windows protected by grilles or shutters?

Garage, outbuildings and grounds
(see pp. 48-9)
– Do all doors and windows have appropriate locks?
– Are all ladders and tools locked away?

– Is the garden free from rubble?

Alarms
(see pp. 50-9)
– Is your property protected by an alarm system?
– Do you test the alarm regularly?
– Do you have a maintenance agreement for your alarm system?

Contents protection
– Have you placed little-used but valuable documents and objects in a bank?
– Do you keep cash, documents and valuable jewellery in a home safe (see pp. 60-1)?
– Is all your property marked with your unique security code (see pp. 62-3)?
– Do you have photographs and a list of serial numbers of your valuable contents?

Fire precautions
(see pp. 66-71)
– Is your home free from fire hazards?

Is your home equipped with:
– smoke alarms?
– fire extinguisher(s)?
– fire blanket?

Household insurance
(see pp 72-5)
– Is your insurance cover up to date?

77

VEHICLE SECURITY

VEHICLE
SECURITY

VEHICLE SECURITY

Auto crime comes top of the list in the number of recorded offences. Despite the fact that a car is often a person's biggest investment outside the home, owners can be dismayingly negligent. An inadequately secured vehicle combines maximum temptation with minimum risk and all too often cars and their contents are left like money

---

Auto crime falls into three categories.

1 **Break-ins** to steal accessories or personal goods account for most auto crime. The preferred targets are entertainment units – car radio/cassette players, speakers, and CB sets – but any item you leave in view, from useless to priceless, invites trouble.

2 **Theft** of the car itself might be for resale, use in another crime, or joyriding. Professionals often steal specific expensive, new, sporty, and rare models to order. Older cars are targets because of the ease of entry and relative anonymity.

3 **Auto vandalism** is as nasty as it is varied. It doesn't take a criminal long to twist the aerial, scratch the paint, shatter the mirrors, or dent a wing.

Although you have a better than even chance of recovering a stolen car, it may well have been damaged in the interim. Evidence suggests that stolen cars have a considerably higher risk of being involved in accidents. The prospects for the return of missing contents are dismal: less than one-tenth are recovered. In monetary terms, the cost of car crime to car owners, even after insurance payouts, can be for-midable, including the expense of alternative transport while a car is missing or being repaired, higher insurance premiums and the loss of no-claims bonus. There is, however, no way to measure the cost in terms of distress and inconvenience.

A determined professional car thief is virtually unstoppable, but unless he has singled out your car for a special reason, he is likely to proceed to a less well-protected one. But remember, professionals account for just a fraction of auto crime; casual thieves commit about 80 per cent of car offences, most of which are preventable.

Protect your car and its contents with the three-step strategy:

1 **Psychological deterrent**
2 **Physical deterrent**
3 **Defence**

PSYCHOLOGICAL DETERRENTS

Use psychological deterrents to discourage an approach or attempted crime. These are mainly commonsense practices that will cost you little or nothing, but will cause the criminal to lose interest. With so many cars to choose from, the criminal will always pick the easiest target; follow these simple rules to make sure it's not yours.

lying in the streets for casual and professional thieves. You can easily reduce your risk of becoming another crime statistic.

ALWAYS:

● **Remove the keys from the ignition** even if you are leaving the car for only a moment, keeping it in sight, or locking it in your garage.

● **Remove or conceal all personal property** even if you know it's worthless. Lock anything you can't remove in the boot or hide it under the shelf in a hatchback. Carry a sheet or blanket in an estate car to cover anything that you have to leave in the car.

● **Close all windows completely**, since even the slightest gap leaves your car wide open to a criminal. Lock the doors, sunroof, and boot or tailgate even in your own driveway or garage.

● **Park in a well-lit area** whenever possible. A dark or secluded spot is the thief's happiest hunting ground and the vandal's safe haven.

REMEMBER!
● *Car thieves work fast! Most auto crime, whether smash-and-grab or outright theft, takes less than a minute.*
● *Don't leave luggage on a roofrack unattended; it can be stolen in seconds.*
● *Never leave children or animals in a parked car. The only way of ensuring them adequate ventilation also creates the risk of theft.*
● *Lower your aerial to reduce the risk of vandalism.*
● *Park with the front wheels turned sharply to reduce the risk of towing.*
● *Watch out for the new British Standard on vehicle security.*

WINDOW ETCHING and LOCKS

WINDOW ETCHING

Window etching is one of the fastest-growing psychological deterrents to car theft. A thief who intends to resell a stolen car knows that he will have the minor expense of changing the number plates to conceal the vehicle's proper identity. However, if you have etched the registration number on each car window, the thief would also have to replace all the glass – an expensive and time-consuming business, and one that could easily arouse suspicion.

Window etching won't prevent vandalism or the theft of valuables from the car, but it is an inexpensive way to discourage theft of the car itself.

You can have your windows etched professionally or you can do it yourself. The professionals prepare a stencil of the number and sand- or bead-blast it onto the windows. Sand-blasting takes about 10 minutes and the result will not impair your visibility or alter the car's appearance.

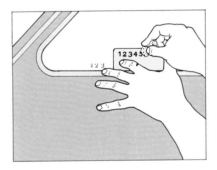

How to etch
You can buy a kit that contains all the materials you need to do your own window etching. Some come with a complete range of stencils for you to compose any number you need, while others offer a pre-formed stencil to order.

You fix the stencil to the window with tape and etch the number with the stylus or apply the chemical etching agent with a brush or an impregnated pad.

LOCKS

The manufacturer's standard locks on new cars offer little challenge to all but the most amateur thief. Even the steering-wheel locks that are now a standard feature on

Door locks
The obvious disadvantage to fitting additional door locks is that, although you have hardened the target effectively, you face the regular inconvenience of needing two keys every time you want to lock or unlock your car.

Secondly, drilling the car doors to fit the extra locks is not a task most owners want to undertake.

You can buy replacement locks that are fitted in the same position as the maker's originals. You must be careful to centre the new lock precisely and avoid leaving a gap around any part of it.

The suitability of replacement locks varies depending on the model of car; some are an easy, perfect fit while others might require some adjustment if the original hole is much larger than the new lock requires.

If you are considering installing replacement locks with a universal fitting, first check that your car has a rod link between the lock and key barrel, and that when you remove the barrel, the hole in the door is round.

Locking wheel nuts
Glamorous accessories are a great lure to petty thieves. A set of locking wheel nuts will protect both wheels and tyres, which can be expensive to replace.

The nuts pose no serious inconvenience to you, since you need to unlock them only on those rare occasions when you need to change a tyre.

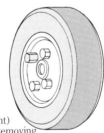

Locking wheel nut (right) and special socket for removing

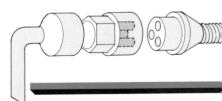

new vehicles do not provide complete protection against theft. Furthermore, because most car manufacturers equip only doors, boot or tailgate, and sunroof with locks, not all the vulnerable areas of your car are protected.

Locking petrol caps
A locking petrol cap is advisable for two reasons. It prevents petrol being siphoned off by thieves, and it prevents vandals from putting things in the petrol tank that can cause the car not to start or to break down.

Combination handbrake lock
This slides over the top of the handbrake lever, locking it in the 'on' position. The lock is keyless; you release it by using a three-digit combination. It can be fitted in minutes to most pull-up type handbrakes and remains in place permanently.

Steering locks
In addition to the standard lock fitted by the manufacturer, you can buy an interior lock. This mechanism hooks on or over the steering wheel and locks it to the brake, accelerator, clutch, or floor-mounted gear stick.

Steering locks vary in quality and may seem a nuisance for short stays, but the very sight of them can deter a thief looking for an easy target.

Choose one that you find easy to operate, as then you will be more likely to use it regularly.

Electronic lock
This anti-theft device prevents the engine from starting until you have entered the correct code on a keypad fixed to the dashboard. If the engine stalls, the unit retains the code for about 10 seconds, allowing you to restart the engine without re-entering the code.

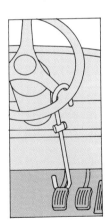

WINDOW ETCHING and LOCKS

REMEMBER!
● *Publicity pays: always use stickers to announce that your car is protected by security measures.*
● *Use your steering-wheel lock: even if it doesn't make the car thief-proof, it slows the criminal down.*
● *Magnetic spare key boxes that fit under the car are a security risk.*
● *Etch your security code on headlamps as well as windows.*

PROFESSIONALLY INSTALLED ALARMS

A car alarm is one of the most effective phychological deterrents. Only a professionally installed system can offer features such as infra-red monitoring and closed-circuit wiring, which provide a higher standard of security than the most sophisticated alarm you install yourself. Having an alarm system fitted by a specialist is your obvious option if you do not have do-it-yourself skills or if you have a particularly expensive

The following features are characteristic of, although not all exclusive to, professionally installed systems:

Passive arming
The system activates itself automatically when you leave the car, so you don't have to rely on your memory. It has pre-set intervals that give you sufficient time to get in or out of the car without setting off the alarm. The system is disarmed by a manually-operated switch concealed under the dashboard.

Security key switch
An external device, usually at the rear of the vehicle, allows you to manually activate and disarm the alarm. Manufacturers supply switches with up to 100 million key variations to ensure security.

Remote control arming/disarming
A radio or infra-red signal from a keyring transmitter turns the system on and off. The car acknowledges receipt of the message by flashing its headlights.

Closed-circuit wiring
This ensures that the alarm will sound even if the cables are tampered with.

Vibration sensors
These detect the high-frequency vibration of forced entry but ignore ordinary traffic flow (see Monitoring opposite).

Back-up battery
The warning system's power supply is independent of the car's battery, which increases its reliability. It can be recharged from the car's electrical system.

Independent audio warning
Sirens, hooters, and other sounders are more distinctive than the car's horn and require less power. Most cut out and reset automatically after a specified interval. Those that sound continuously can contravene the Control of Pollution Act and therefore are not recommended. Some systems also incorporate a remote-warning pager. Although these may be sold in Britain, it is against the law to use them.

Immobilization
Simultaneous with sounding a warning, the system blocks key electrical circuits, such as ignition.

Modular system
Selected components from specialist outlets are combined to produce a custom-made system for an individual vehicle.

Fail-safe dual circuit
Two methods of monitoring are incorporated into the alarm system (see Monitoring opposite).

Self-test system
The alarm is continuously self-monitored to ensure it is working properly.

car. Getting what you pay for should include fine and unobtrusive workmanship as well as reliable after-sales service.

MONITORING

There are various methods of detecting tampering or entry and activating the warning.

Voltage-drop sensor

The most basic method. The system constantly monitors its own voltage level.

The alarm is activated when the voltage drops suddenly, for example when the car door is opened and the courtesy lights come on or the key is put in the ignition and the dashboard lights up. Also called current-drain sensor.

Earth-seeking sensor

Pin-switches (door contacts) are fitted everywhere entry or tampering is likely: doors, bonnet, boot or tailgate.

Opening a point where a switch is fitted releases the pin, which electrically earths the system and sets off the alarm.

Motion detection facility

Sensors, switches or circuits are used to detect the car being rocked, jolted, jacked up, or towed.

● The trembler switch consists of a ball-bearing sitting between two contacts. The alarm sounds when movement, such as a door being opened, causes the ball-bearing to touch the contact.

● The vibrator contact circuit (also called an adjustable impact device) has a relatively light weight on the end of a piece of spring metal, with a contact under the weight. When the spring metal vibrates, the weight touches the contact, activating the alarm. Sensitivity is controlled by adjusting the distance between the weight and the contact.

● An ultrasonic sensor continuously monitors the inaudible high-frequency sound waves it transmits and receives.

The alarm is activated when the pattern is disturbed, for example, by a window being smashed or a soft-top being cut.

ROOFRACKS AND TRAILERS

These particularly vulnerable areas can be armed with a remote sensor wire alarm.

PROFESSIONALLY INSTALLED ALARMS

Ultrasonic sensor

REMEMBER!

● *Display an alarm sticker whether or not your car has an alarm system. Most casual thieves won't test its authenticity, but will move on to another target.*

● *Don't wait to protect your car. More than half the professionally-installed alarms are sold to people who are already victims of auto crime.*

DIY CAR ALARMS

Any alarm system is better than none, and do-it-yourself alarms can provide security for contents by deterring criminals or frightening them off mid-job. The obvious advantage of a DIY car alarm system is the cost. The main disadvantages are as follows:

● Most cannot be passively armed, so you must remember to turn it on when you leave the car.

● Because most car alarms rely on the car horn for the warning noise, it is possible that the battery will run down.

● People might think the noise is a malfunction rather than evidence of criminal tampering.

To overcome these last two points, you can fit an independent siren or horn, which has a distinctive sound, uses only a fraction of the power of a car horn, and can be fixed in a position less vulnerable to prying hands.

MONITORING

Most DIY systems monitor entry by voltage-drop sensors activated when the car door is opened and the courtesy lights come on, or earth-seeking sensors (see pp. 84-5) on the doors, bonnet, boot, sunroof, and accessories. Because a voltage-drop system does not cover all potential points of entry and will not function if your courtesy lights are not working, it is best to reinforce it with earth-seeking sensors or an ultrasonic unit.

The latter fills the car interior with a steady self-monitored pattern of inaudible high-frequency sound waves. If the pattern is disturbed, for example, by a door being opened or a window smashed, the unit activates the voltage-drop sensors and the alarm sounds.

CHOOSING AND FITTING A CAR ALARM

You tend to get what you pay for in terms of sophistication and convenience, so in choosing a kit, weigh up what you want to

THE KIT COMPONENTS
Although kit contents vary according to price, the basic components are: switch-activated sensors to monitor entry; an internal or external switch to arm the system and the key to operate it (external switches should be supplied with spring covers to protect them from dirt and corrosion); the necessary wiring; full instructions.

Many kits include a sticker stating that the car is protected by an alarm.

The most rudimentary system is a voltage-drop or earth-seeking monitor connected to the car's horn.

It is essential that you choose one with a cut-out and reset function to avoid a flat battery and furious neighbours.

The most

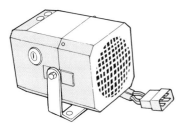

Independent siren

INSTALLATION GUIDELINES
● Read the instructions several times before you begin work to be sure that you understand them.

Relate them to your car so that you can properly identify the wires. Refer to your car handbook for coding.

● Do not attempt the job unless you have all the proper tools.
● Check the length of the wires supplied in the kit by tying them together at the front of the car and extending them to the rear, allowing for curves. If they are not long enough, you can buy more wire.
● If the car horn is to be the audio warning, establish whether it is live-fed or earth-fed.

spend against the degree of protection you expect. You must also bear in mind your own level of skill in wiring and fitting. Ask to read the instructions supplied with the kit *before* you buy to make sure you will be able to do the work.

DIY CAR ALARMS

comprehensive system might include inertia sensors, an ultrasonic unit and an independent siren.

Most kits include an ignition cut-out that automatically immobilizes the car when the alarm is activated.

Alternatively, you can also buy an engine immobilizer and fit it with an alarm.

Often the more expensive kits are easier to install. Some require only two wires to be connected, and some do without wires entirely.

One system that doesn't require you to drill holes combines a dashboard-mounted keypad switch that you arm and disarm with a personal code, and a vibration-sensitive diode to activate the siren.

Some kit manufacturers offer additional parts that are compatible with the basic kit system.

If you think you might want to increase your level of security later, start with a system that offers this flexibility.

Options might include a circuit that flashes the headlights on and off, a coded keypad, and an entry/exit delay.

REMEMBER!

No system is so good that it can compensate for bad fitting. If you're going to do it yourself, get it right the first time.

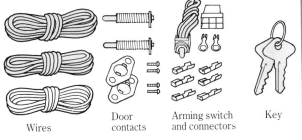

| Wires | Door contacts | Arming switch and connectors | Key |

● Disconnect the battery before you start work.
● Decide where the holes need to be drilled and complete all the drilling before taking the next step.
● Work as neatly as possible, routing the wires to avoid chafing, using insulating tape and the car's loom clips to keep them tidy and safe.

● Wherever wires have to pass through metal, use grommets to prevent chafing.
● Use proper connectors for wiring connections and make sure they are tight; poor connections are the commonest cause of systems malfunctioning.

● Locate the control box under the bonnet in a clean, dry, flat place. Position it so that the loom run is as short as possible and screw it securely to the bulkhead.
● Locate the exterior key switch in a double-skinned panel or in the boot area so that the back of it can't be reached when the car is locked.

87

IMMOBILIZATION

It is possible that a thief will get into your car even if you have heeded all the advice about psychological and physical deterrents given in the preceding pages. If this does happen, your final defence against theft of the vehicle is immobilization. A car that can't be moved quickly and easily loses its appeal – and when an effective form of immobilization is obviously in use, it also acts as a powerful deterrent.

There are two categories of immobilization: electrical and mechanical. The very

ELECTRICAL IMMOBILIZATION

DISTRIBUTOR
You can quickly snap off the distributor cap and remove the T-shaped rotor arm sitting in the middle of the distributor. It's small enough to put in a handbag or pocket, or you can lock it in the boot. Few thieves carry a spare rotor arm with them!

The only disadvantage is that it can be messy and inconvenient if you are leaving the car for only a short time.

SPARK PLUGS
Simply swap over or remove a couple of the plug leads.

IGNITION
Disabler switch
Supplied in simple DIY kits, this switch is usually hidden under the dashboard and interrupts the ignition feed wire. If the interruption is made between the battery and the coil, a thief can still easily 'hot wire' the car to start it; but if the interruption is made between the coil and the distributor, he can't.

Passively-armed cut-out
This device renders the ignition dead as soon as you switch it off. When you want to start the car again, you deactivate the cut-out by depressing a button or switch while you start the engine.

Printed circuit card
The card slots into a socket mounted on the dashboard. When you take the card out it breaks vital electrical circuits.

ELECTRIC FUEL PUMP
Another way to defeat the possibility of hot-wiring is to fit a switch that interrupts the feed wire to the electric fuel pump.

MULTIPLE CUT-OUT
The central control box in an electrical alarm or non-alarmed anti-theft system is bolted to the bulkhead under the bonnet and disrupts several electrical circuits at the same time.

MECHANICAL IMMOBILIZATION

Steering locks (see also pp. 82-3).
You can buy a robust additional lock that fits around the steering column like an armoured collar. The lock key then replaces the vehicle ignition key and controls the electrical operations. This lock will deter the casual criminal, but a well-equipped thief will use one tool to pull out the guts of the lock and another to clamp around the column and sheer off the lock pins.

Wheel clamp
This may seem an extreme measure, and it certainly is a nuisance to fit and remove on a regular basis, but it is effective. One wheel clamp prevents your car from being driven or towed away, even if the tyre is deflated. Most have the added advantage of preventing the tyre and wheel from being removed by making it impossible to reach the wheel nuts (see also pp. 82-3). This type of clamp is a good investment if you leave your car unattended or ungaraged for long periods.

simplest devices will probably discourage most joyriders, but a routine ignition cut-out or standard steering-wheel lock is child's play to the streetwise car thief. However, there are ways to stop him, too.

PROTECTION FOR CAR ACCESSORIES

Sound systems are the thief's favourite target. There are a number of ways to protect your radio-cassette player.
● Fit the system with alarm switches. However, if it has no other protection, a thief who has got inside the vehicle will have committed himself and the unit might be damaged.
● Use a cassette lock. This device is inserted like a normal cassette, but locks into place and is impossible to remove without the key, rendering the player useless.
  A large tag hanging from the lock states that the system is protected, and window stickers are also available.
● Install a computer-coded system that will work only when the correct code is entered using the control buttons.
● Use a portable radio-cassette that slides into a permanently fixed pre-wired sleeve or quick-release mounting bracket. You can easily remove the set whenever you leave the car, and carry it with you or lock it in the boot.

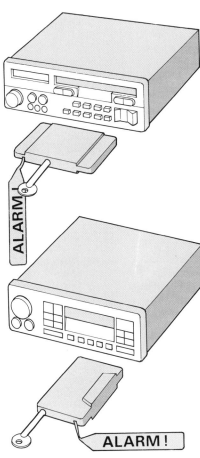

Cassette locks

IMMOBILIZATION

REMEMBER!
● *The simplest do-it-yourself method of protection is to remove the rotor arm from the distributor.*
● *By locking or removing your car sound system, you not only protect your property from theft, but also remove many a thief's main incentive for breaking in.*

BICYCLES and MOTORCYCLES

Not so long ago bicycles were used mainly by children for amusement and transport. Today, because of public concern about physical fitness and air pollution, bicycles are increasingly popular among adults.

They are also big business for thieves, who respond to the law of supply and demand for two-wheelers as readily as for cars.

Mountain bikes, touring bikes and racers are trendy and expensive, but even if

BICYCLES

● Insure your bicycle. You might be offered a special policy through the shop where you buy the bike, or you can add it to your household insurance policy.
● Mark the bicycle. Many new bicycles do not come with a serial number stamped on the frame, so devise a code and do it yourself. Be sure to display a 'coded cycle' sticker. This is a simple but extremely effective deterrent: surveys have shown that given a choice between a marked and an unmarked bike, thieves will take the latter. Coding also greatly increases your chances of having a stolen bicycle returned.

The most effective code is your house number and postal code. You can hire a metal die stamp to inscribe the code somewhere on the bicycle frame, such as the bottom bracket (not recommended for aluminium frames). Consult your local police to see if they offer this service.
● Keep a record. Make a note of the bicycle's serial number or the code you have stamped on the frame and every distinguishing characteristic that could help identify it, such as make, frame style, colour, saddle, tyres, damage and dimensions. Keeping a clear photograph is also advisable.

MOTORCYCLES

Thieves steal motorcycles for resale and for spare parts. The top-of-the-range new models and virtually irreplaceable classics are obvious targets. Professional thieves, usually working in pairs and formidably equipped, regularly take the bikes of their choice in broad daylight in less than a minute.

Like a car, a motorcycle can be electrically immobilized and – although it is uncommon – fitted with an alarm. It also has a number plate and serial number to identify it. Like a bicycle, its main form of protection is a chain and padlock.

The law requiring motorcyclists to wear a crash helmet is an excellent deterrent to the casual thief. He might see an unsecured bike, but without a helmet, he risks immediate trouble from the police.

Always take your helmet with you even if your bike has a helmet lock on the frame;

the helmet can easily be released by cutting through the chin strap. At the least only your expensive helmet will be stolen, and at the worst it will become an accessory to the theft of your bike.

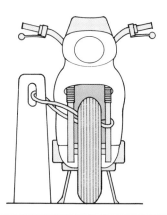

you are concerned only with an old boneshaker or a child's BMX, it is essential to take basic precautions.

SECURING YOUR BICYCLE

Bike chain lock
This is your only real defence. Use a heavy-duty chain sheathed in plastic and a stout padlock or wire hawser lock.
Use hardened steel products because bolt-croppers can cut through anything softer.

At home
Keep your bike in a locked building or garage, chained to a secure fixture.

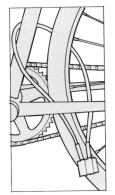

Accessories
If you must leave your bike for long periods, be sure to strip it of lights (unless they are attached with security bolts), panniers and pump.

Extra measure
Removing the front wheel is not as difficult as it sounds if you have a quick-release fitting, and is a first-rate deterrent.

SECURING YOUR MOTORCYCLE

Locks
Buy a high quality padlock and chain or wire rope with a written guarantee, or buy a specially designed padlock with hardened elongated shackles that pass through the forks and front wheel.
Use your steering lock, but don't depend on it alone: one fierce wrench of the handle-bars can break it.

Alarms and disablers
You can fit an audio alarm with its own battery, but its effectiveness as a deterrent is doubtful.

To immobilize your bike, remove the battery earth strap or the line-fuse in the main lead near the battery terminals.
Or fit a concealed cut-out switch that breaks any of the low-tension wires to the coil.

At home
Keep the bike in a locked garage or shed, or locked to a post that is bolted, screwed, or cemented into the ground.
Some people who live for their bikes wheel them indoors at night, but this is not always practical.

Extra measures
If you leave your motorcycle for long periods, you can take the following steps:
● Fit unserviceable but visibly complete spark plugs;
● Drain the float chambers and remove or block the fuel supply line;
● Select first gear and remove the gear and clutch levers.

Accessories
Remove panniers and top boxes that are not bolted in place.
Lock boxes and panniers that are bolted in place.

BICYCLES and MOTORCYCLES

REMEMBER!
● *Always pass the chain through the frame and wheel, and lock it to an immovable object. On a bicycle, don't chain the wheel alone, or it might be all you find when you return.*
● *Use your lock and chain no matter how briefly you leave your bike. It can be stolen in seconds.*
● *If you are out as one of a group, consider chaining and locking all your bicycles together.*
● *On the street, cover a motorbike with a heavy waterproof sheet padlocked into place.*
● *Park in well-lit, open places.*
● *Avoid leaving a motorcycle parked in the same place for more than two days in a row; it is small enough to be power-lifted into a waiting truck.*

CAMPERS, CARAVANS and BOATS

These vehicles and vessels call for security measures appropriate to both houses and cars. Like houses, they may contain appliances, tools, audio and video equipment – and in boats, specialist equipment such as radar – and need to have all access points secured to prevent entry. Like cars, they must be immobilized to prevent removal. At home or at the marina, on the road or on the water, there are some simple precautions you can take.

SECURING YOUR CAMPER OR CARAVAN

Deterrents
● Never leave valuable items on view.

At home, if it is to be unused for some time, strip it internally and leave empty drawers open. Leave the curtains open to show that nothing is inside.

On the road close the curtains when you are out to reduce temptation.
● Replace original locks on doors, windows, and sunroof with special security locks.

● Etch the window glass with your registration or chassis number and display warning stickers. You can also die-stamp the number on the wheels or paint it inconspicuously on the roof or underside to aid in identification.
● Try not to park in a deserted area.
● Always set the alarm and immobilize the vehicle when you are going out even for a short time.

Alarms
DIY kits contain a control unit, audio warning, point-of-entry switches, an anti-tilt or motion detection sensor, a junction box, and wire.

Some come with rechargeable batteries; others rely on the car battery, which can be used in caravans only when touring, or on mains power, which is useful only in permanently sited, static caravans or campsites with

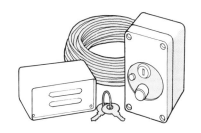

SECURING YOUR BOAT

At home
● Chain and padlock the craft to the trailer.
● Immobilize the trailer with a wheel clamp (see pp. 88-9) or hitchlock (see above).
● Remove all portable equipment, such as oars, oarlocks, and outboard motors.
● Keep the boat and trailer chained to a secure fixture in a locked garage or shed.

On the water
● Do not moor up with rope alone. Chain your boat and use the best weatherproof padlocks available.
● Identify tenders with the mother vessel's name and your own security code.
● Do the same for surf and sailboards, inflatables and canoes, and chain and padlock them to roofracks when in transit.

Outboard motors
● Keep a record of the make and serial number.
● Etch or die stamp your security code on it.

● Always remove it when not in use *or* chain lock or bolt it in place and shroud the securing nuts with a lock (see below).

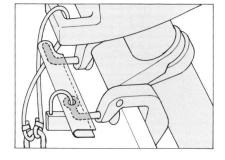

CAMPERS, CARAVANS and BOATS

electric power outlets.

An external siren can be heard best, but must be tamperproof and weatherproof.

Place an indoor siren near an air vent for maximum effectiveness.

Immobilization
● Use a wheel clamp (see pp. 88-9).

Extra measures for a caravan
● Jack it up and remove a wheel.

● Use a dummy ball that locks into the hitch socket, or a hitch lock that covers the socket.

● Drill a hole in the chassis near a wheel. Thread a plastic-sheathed chain through both and secure with a brass padlock.
● Hitch it to a secure shackle post using either the post's integral lock or a high-quality chain and padlock.
● Fit locks to the rear caravan stays to prevent them from being raised.

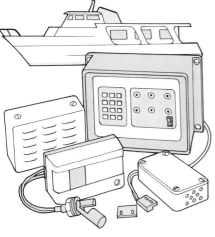

Cruisers and luxury craft
● Keep valuables out of sight or bolted in place.
● Install security locks on doors, hatches, and windows.
● Install an alarm that will not be activated by the wind or tide.

Use a system with a battery that can withstand long periods of discharge when the boat is not in use or can be linked to the marina's office or security company's control room.

REMEMBER!
● *The sudden absence of a camper, caravan, or boat normally parked in public view outside your home announces your departure, so make sure you secure your house properly before you leave (see pp. 98-9).*
● *Keep a lookout at the marina. A good marina should have a security guard; know who he is and inform him if you see anything suspicious.*
● *Form a waterside Neighbourhood Watch if you moor on a river or in a harbour away from a marina.*

CAR FIRES

A fire can start anywhere there is a source of ignition, combustible material, and air. A car is particularly inflammable. Electrical sparks, engine heat, or the friction of metal on metal or metal on road all have the potential to ignite. Petrol is the most combustible substance in a car, but oil, rubber, fabric, plastic and paintwork will burn too.

The chief cause of car fires is poor maintenance; the result is at the least smelly and destructive, and at the worst, fatal.

PREVENTION

Wiring
If you install your own accessories or car alarm system, be very careful. Use the following materials:
- Rubber grommets, to avoid wires chafing.
- Solder or insulated connectors to link wires, not tape, which deteriorates.
- Recommended grades of wire only.
- The correct fuses.
Never bridge a fuse that blows repeatedly; find the fault causing it and repair it.

Fuel lines
Check all fuel lines for brittleness and replace any that are cracked or split. Secure them with clips at every connection. Check the tank and outlet stub for corrosion. A fuel system inertia switch cuts off the flow of petrol on impact.

Never touch the fuel system until the engine has cooled.

Petrol odours
Investigate odours immediately to isolate the source – leaking under the bonnet, carburettor spilling, float level too high, spare can leaking.

Battery
Always disconnect the battery when you are working under the bonnet. A battery master switch breaks the connection with a quick-release clamp, which is also useful in case of fire. To prevent an explosion, never expose the battery to a naked flame or even a lighted cigarette.

Air filter
Will reduce the risk of toxic fumes.

FIRE EXTINGUISHERS

Carry the largest fire extinguisher that fits in your car.

Keep it mounted on a bracket (sometimes supplied by the manufacturer) in a readily accessible position in the front of the car, out of direct sunlight.

Take note of the shelf life and follow any maintenance instructions.

You can also install a heat-sensitive automatic extinguisher under the bonnet.

There are two main types of extinguisher.

Halon-BCF
(Bromochlorodifluoromethane) This halts combustion chemically and vaporizes, leaving no residue. It is the most widely used extinguishant.

Dry powder
This type of extinguisher can be used on fires involving spilt liquids, such as oil and petrol.

IN CASE OF FIRE

If you see or smell smoke, don't panic. Pull off the road, keeping as clear as possible of other cars and pedestrians.

Fires following collision
Fire is often caused when fuel is sprayed over a hot engine (see Fuel lines, left).
- Get everyone clear of the vehicle.
- Call the fire brigade.

Interior fires
Electrical shorts are often the cause of fires breaking out under or behind the dashboard.
- Get out of the car.
- Lean in to turn off the ignition and the lights.
- Use the fire extinguisher.
- If time allows, disconnect the battery (see Battery, left).

CAR FIRES

Both types are available in total discharge (single use) and controllable discharge (repeat use) dispensers.

The latter costs more, but it is good to have some left over in case the first attempt isn't totally effective.

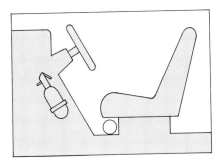

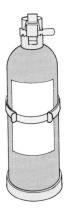

Under-bonnet fires
● Release the bonnet to its lowest position, keeping air exposure to a minimum.
● Protecting your hand with a rag or cloth, aim the fire extinguisher into the gap and release the contents until the flames subside.
● Wait a few minutes, then spray some more extinguishant into the gap before opening the bonnet completely. Cover your nose and mouth with a cloth or handkerchief and try not to inhale the fumes.

REMEMBER!
● *Extinguish cigarettes completely.*
● *Never leave matches or a lighter in the car with children.*

THE WARY
TRAVELLER

THE WARY TRAVELLER

Whenever you are travelling, there are three aspects of security you must consider: the home you are leaving; the money, baggage and personal effects you are carrying in transit; and your accommodation. When you travel take the least you can manage with, carry a separate record of your valuables, and follow many of the same practices you do at home. Before leaving, minimize all signs of your absence. Travel may be your luxury; don't make it the criminal's opportunity.

LUGGAGE

Choose suitcases not only for their appearance and convenience, but also for the security they offer. Suitcases are subject to varying degrees of wear and tear depending on their construction and the means of transport. Soft-sided cases can tear easily, and cases of glass-fibre shell construction can split when dropped on a hard surface. Generally, quality is related to price.

The average suitcase deteriorates more quickly if used for air travel rather than rail, car or coach travel because it is subjected to much rougher handling and conditions during loading and unloading. Insurers recommend aluminium flight cases as the most robust. Check the condition of your luggage and have any necessary repairs made after every trip so that your suitcases will always be in good condition for the next time you need them.

Locks
Anything that threatens to delay the thief may deter him.
● Always use the locks on your suitcases.
● Padlock zips on soft-sided cases.
● Check that all locks are in good working order before and after each trip.
● Use luggage straps. They may deter a thief and provide extra security if the suitcase clasps spring open.

PACKING

Use your common sense when packing. Pack only clothes in the luggage that will not be in your care during the journey. Be sure you remove cufflinks and brooches from garments and check all pockets for valuables. Never overfill a suitcase, since this can make it rupture during handling.

Carry in hand luggage or on your person any items of great value, such as jewellery, cameras, cash and travellers' cheques (see pp. 104-5), credit cards, passport and other documents.

PRECAUTIONS
● Estimate the value of your luggage and its contents. Compare this to the maximum your insurance or the airline will pay for lost luggage. Take out additional insurance if necessary.
● Make and carry separately a list of what is in your luggage so you can make an insurance claim if your bags are lost.
● Professional burglars frequent airports and terminals looking at labels for the home addresses of people going away.
● Label your bags outside with your destination.
● Put your home address only inside the cases.
● Lock your cases and carry a spare set of keys.
● Pack toiletries and a change of clothing in your hand luggage in case your cases are lost or delayed.

Jewellery
● Leave valuable jewellery at home in a safe or safe deposit box, and carry only the costume variety.
● If you must carry some valuable pieces, always keep them in a locked box. Put the box in your handbag or hand luggage and deposit it in the hotel safe on your arrival.

NEVER:
● Put jewellery in a suitcase.
● Leave jewellery lying out in a hotel room.
● Leave jewellery *anywhere* in a car.
● Wear jewellery to the beach.

Documents
● Leave at home all documents unrelated to your journey, such as local charge cards and library cards.

● Record the numbers of all credit cards and documents, such as passport and driving licence, you are taking with you.
● Keep your copy separate from your purse or wallet, and leave a copy, plus your itinerary, with someone at home. If you suffer a loss, this will make replacement easier and limit your liability.

REMEMBER!
● *Light is right: the less you take, the less you risk. Don't take anything you don't really need.*
● *Your hands might swell during a flight or sudden change to a warmer climate. If you have to remove your rings, put them somewhere safe immediately.*
● *Don't leave a message on your telephone answering machine stating that you are away.*
● *Don't allow newspapers to run a feature if you win a trip.*
● *Check that automatic timers for lights, radio, etc. are working.*
● *Switch on the burglar alarm before you go!*

PROTECTING YOUR HOME

Before you leave, do everything possible to disguise your absence and make your home secure (see *Home Safe*).

● Cancel all regular deliveries, such as milk and newspapers.

● Leave a spare set of keys with someone you trust. Ask them to collect post and leaflets, mow the grass, park in your driveway or move your car and generally provide a lived-in look.

● Advise local police of your absence, where to contact you and the holder of your spare keys.

● Leave no valuables on view through the windows. Put your most precious things in a safe or store them at the bank.

● Close and lock all windows and doors as you leave, and close the front gate.

TRANSPORT and PUBLIC PLACES

Travel – especially while you are in transit – can be disorientating. Airports, train stations, coach terminals and hotel lobbies are the hunting grounds of thieves and pickpockets, who take advantage of the weariness, preoccupation and momentary confusion that often make people more vulnerable away from home. You need to keep your wits about you and be vigilant to avoid theft or accidental loss. Plan your time so that you do not have to rush, which often results in carelessness.

TRANSPORT

At a terminal
● When you travel by air, make sure that the correct destination label is put on your case by airline staff at the check-in desk.
● When you travel by coach, make sure your luggage is stored in the hold before you take your seat.
● If you require help with your luggage, use only legitimate porters – identifiable by uniforms or badges – and agree charges before the cases are moved.

NEVER:
● Let your bags out of your sight, not even for a moment. Always keep your eye on your luggage when using the telephone, the lavatory or the bank; making purchases, eating or drinking.
● Ask strangers, no matter how nice or honest they seem, to look after your bags.
● Agree to look after a stranger's luggage.
● Agree to transport a package or any luggage for a stranger; it might contain anything from contraband to explosives.

In transit
● If you want to sleep, use your handbag as a pillow or tuck it securely between yourself and the seat.

● Before you disembark, check that you have all your belongings.

INTERNATIONAL AIRPORT CODES

Alicante	ALC	Madrid	MAD
Amsterdam	AMS	Majorca	PMA
Athens	ATH	Manchester	MAN
Barcelona	BCN	Montreal	YUL
Brussels	BRU	New York	
Dublin	DUB	Kennedy	JFK
Edinburgh	EDI	Newark	EWR
Frankfurt	FRA	Paris	
Geneva	GVA	De Gaulle	CDG
Hong Kong	HKG	Orly	ORY
Limerick	SNM	Rome	FCO
London		Sydney	SYD
Heathrow	LHR	Tokyo	TYO
Gatwick	LGW	Toronto	YYZ
Los Angeles	LAX	Vienna	VIA

TRANSPORT
and PUBLIC
PLACES

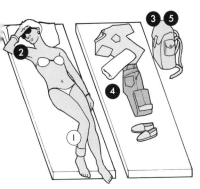

PUBLIC
PLACES

On the beach and
by the pool

1 Carry cash, keys or cards in a small waterproof pouch that you can wear around your neck, wrist or ankle.
2 Don't bring or wear jewellery.
3 Don't leave any valuables unattended.
4 Don't reserve deck chairs by leaving your personal property on them.
5 Don't ask a stranger to look after your belongings while you go for a swim.

In the car

● Whether the car is your own or a rented one, don't risk having it broken into or stolen.
● Park in a well-lit, active area if possible.
● Lock all windows and doors every time you get out.
● Don't leave any valuables in the car. Lock anything you cannot carry in the boot, preferably before you park.
● See also *Vehicle Security.*

Out and about

● Ask at your hotel about recommended areas and trouble spots to avoid.
● Know and abide by the customs and standards regarding dress and behaviour when visiting a foreign country.

　Ignoring local rules may result in expulsion from public buildings or places of worship, unfriendly behaviour by the local people, or even arrest and deportation.

● Plan ahead what you will do with your handbag if you go dancing.
● Don't carry money, credit cards or other valuables in your camera case.
● Think about drink. Alcohol makes you more vulnerable to muggers and pickpockets, so either limit your consumption or take a taxi back to your hotel after an evening out.

REMEMBER!

● *Always report unattended luggage or parcels to the nearest official.*
● *Luggage can vanish in seconds: awareness is your best defence.*
● *In crowds, professional thieves work in teams: one distracts while another steals, and a third takes away the stolen goods.*
● *Suspect any 'accidental' contact with strangers.*
● *Use only licensed, metered taxis.*

101

YOUR HOME away from HOME

It is in any hotel's interest that no crime is committed against you on its premises. The level of security in hotels varies greatly; the larger and more expensive hotels tend to employ professional security staff. However, most hotels display signs in public areas and individual rooms limiting their liability. Final responsibility for valuables always remains with the guest.

Take the same basic precautions you do

SECURITY

Hotels

1 If you plan to take jewellery or other valuables with you, check in advance that the hotel you are booked at offers a safe deposit facility.

2 Immediately after checking in, familiarize yourself with the fire exits near your room and elsewhere on your floor. This could save your life if there is a power failure or if dense smoke created by a fire impairs your visibility.

3 Always lock your door when you are in your room. Never leave the door ajar, however briefly.

4 Never open the door unless you know who the caller is. If the caller claims to be making a delivery or repairs, get confirmation from the desk first.

5 Always lock your door when you leave your room. If it locks automatically, give it a strong push and pull to make sure it has closed securely.

6 Check how your windows and door to the balcony, verandah or patio operate and where they lead. Always lock them at night and when you leave the room.

7 Don't advertise your absence by leaving signs for the staff to clean the room or messages for friends on your door.

8 When you go out, lodge any valuables you don't want to carry in the hotel's safe deposit.

9 Report any suspicious behaviour to hotel security.

10 On departure do not leave packed luggage in your room unattended; you could be robbed without knowing it until you unpacked at your destination. If you must leave packed luggage, ask the hotel to lock it in the security room.

11 Leave your key with the front desk whenever you leave your room. This reduces the risk that you might lose it – and a thief find it – in a bar or restaurant, at the beach or by the pool.

12 At night, keep your key on the beside table.

Motels

● Keep your room locked whether you are in or out. Keep curtains drawn after dark and when you are out.

● See also *Vehicle Security*.

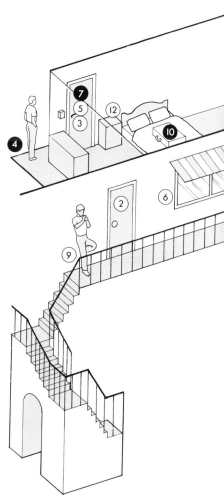

at home, and make use of the hotel safe. Security measures won't spoil your time away; in fact, they should make it easier for you to relax and enjoy yourself.

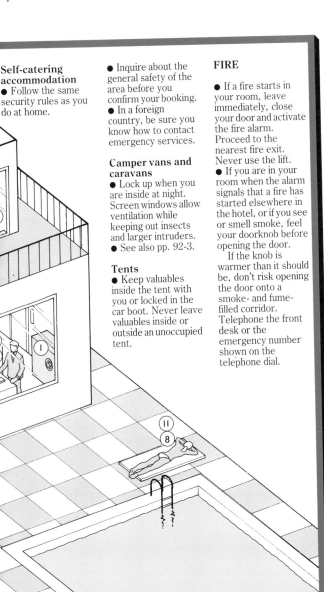

Self-catering accommodation
● Follow the same security rules as you do at home.

● Inquire about the general safety of the area before you confirm your booking.
● In a foreign country, be sure you know how to contact emergency services.

Camper vans and caravans
● Lock up when you are inside at night. Screen windows allow ventilation while keeping out insects and larger intruders.
● See also pp. 92-3.

Tents
● Keep valuables inside the tent with you or locked in the car boot. Never leave valuables inside or outside an unoccupied tent.

FIRE
● If a fire starts in your room, leave immediately, close your door and activate the fire alarm. Proceed to the nearest fire exit. Never use the lift.
● If you are in your room when the alarm signals that a fire has started elsewhere in the hotel, or if you see or smell smoke, feel your doorknob before opening the door.
  If the knob is warmer than it should be, don't risk opening the door onto a smoke- and fume-filled corridor. Telephone the front desk or the emergency number shown on the telephone dial.

YOUR HOME
away from
HOME

REMEMBER!
● *Your safety and that of your property is your responsibility.*
● *Always keep valuables in the hotel safe.*
● *Never disclose your home address to strangers you meet on holiday.*

MONEY on the MOVE

Cash is the thief's number one target at home and abroad. Carry only as much cash – in your own currency and that of any foreign country you may be visiting – as you need for taxis, telephones and light refreshments and other casual expenditures. Use cheques, travellers' cheques and credit cards.

Handle all forms of money discreetly. Unfamiliarity with foreign currency makes

TRAVELLERS' CHEQUES

Travellers' cheques present less risk than cash when you are travelling abroad because they can be replaced if lost.

ALWAYS

● Follow the instructions issued with the cheques.

● Record the serial numbers of your cheques on the slip provided.

● Keep this slip separate from the cheques as instructed, and cross off the serial numbers when you use the cheques. If the cheques are stolen, you will then have an accurate list of the missing ones.

● Insist that other people travelling with you carry their own travellers' cheques.

CREDIT CARDS

Credit cards minimize the amount of cash you need to carry. Your copies of the sales vouchers act as proof of purchase, which is useful if you need to make an insurance claim or replace lost airline tickets. Major card companies also offer free travel insurance if you use your card to purchase airline tickets.

PROTECTING YOUR MONEY

Don't carry all your funds in one place; allocate some to a secure pocket, some to a secure bag. Keep your chequebook and cheque card separate.

Pockets
● Side pockets of jackets and trousers are risky, and back trouser pockets are the main target of pickpockets.
● An inside jacket pocket that buttons, zips or fastens by other means is more secure.

Money belts
1 A zipped money belt worn under your clothes is the most secure way to carry valuables.
2 A smaller alternative is a pouch large enough to hold a passport, a few credit cards, tickets and some currency.

One type has a loop for threading on your belt and is worn flipped over the inside of your waistband.
3 Others are worn on your wrist or ankle, or on a cord around your neck under your clothes.
4 The smallest alternative is a cord-hung capsule that is large enough only for small amounts of cash.

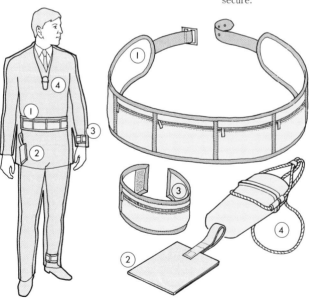

people treat it like Monopoly money. It's not. It's real, so take good care of it and don't flash it around.

Bags

- A basket or handbag that is open at the top is an easy target for thieves.
- A clutch bag or a handbag with a strong clasp is more secure if you carry it carefully.
- A shoulder bag with a zip closing is more secure than one with only a flap. Carry the latter with the flap toward your body.

Always carry a shoulder bag at your side, never hanging at your back.

Wear a shoulder bag on the shoulder away from traffic to protect yourself from scooter thieves. They work in pairs – as they speed past, one drives and the other grabs the bag by the strap.

If you try to hold on to the bag, the thief might be pulled off the bike or you might be thrown to the ground.

Out and about

- Remove all valuables – cards, cash, keys – from your coat or jacket before leaving it in a cloakroom or hanging it on a coat rack in a public place.
- Don't leave handbags or jackets unattended for even a moment when trying on clothes or shoes in a shop.

1 Never hang a handbag or jacket over your chair.

2 Never put a handbag on the floor by your chair. Keep it between your feet or on your lap.

3 Never put loose change, hotel keys or lighters on a bar or table in a public place.

- Check that your credit card has been returned to you before leaving a shop or restaurant. Make sure it is *your* card, not a stolen one that has been substituted.
- Save your credit card receipts. A carelessly discarded copy can be used to make charges by telephone and to falsify a card.
- Always put cards, cheques and cash away immediately after use.
- Be wary in crowds. Thieves thrive wherever jostlings seem natural.

If you feel any contact being made, drop your arms and turn round as quickly as possible in case a pickpocket is at work.

Discreetly check your valuables are where they should be.

MONEY on the MOVE

REMEMBER!

- *Never carry money or jewellery in your camera case.*
- *Be careful in open air markets where haggling is popular: your pocket can be picked while you are being distracted.*
- *Avoid close contact and conversations with strangers. Pickpockets often work as teams, one distracting you while the others steal.*
- *In a foreign country change money only at accredited banks, bureaux de change, or your hotel, which will supply receipts verifying rates and charges.*

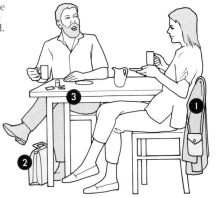

INSURANCE

If you are travelling within your own country, you usually do not need special travel insurance. Check your household policy to see if you have all-risks coverage for property or money lost or stolen outside the home. This is also the best way to insure items of high value when you travel abroad, because the coverage for baggage, personal effects and money offered by the average travel insurance policy is very limited. Always read the fine print to avoid disappointment later.

GENERAL TRAVEL POLICIES

Travel insurance policies have a standard format, but differ in the coverage they offer. The premiums vary according to the areas visited, the duration of travel and, in some cases, planned activities, such as winter sports, underwater sports, potholing and mountaineering.

Most policies insure against the following occurrences.
● Personal accident.
● Medical expenses.
● Loss or damage of baggage, personal effects and money.
● Travel delay.
● Personal liability.
● Travel cancellation.

All policies exlude any liability in the event of natural disaster, acts of terrorism or war.

Before accepting a policy, read all the fine print in every section, and make sure you understand the terms to which you are agreeing. Make sure that the total allowance for the property that is at risk of being lost, stolen or damaged, as well as the separate ceilings for individual items and for cash, is adequate for your needs. Check the exclusion clauses to find out how much of each claim is deductible.

If you are travelling on a package holiday, insurance might be included in the price or offered as an extra. You can also obtain policies through a travel agent, insurance broker or the main clearing banks.

MEDICAL INSURANCE

Britain has a reciprocal health care arrangement with the EEC (excluding France and Greece), which entitles you to free medical treatment.

You must complete form E111 at the local office of the Department of Social Security before you travel and present the form when you need treatment. The form is valid for two years.

Take out medical cover, usually available as part of a general travel insurance policy, if you are planning to travel in France, Greece or any country outside the EEC, especially the United States.

CAR INSURANCE

If you are taking your car abroad, apply to your insurance broker for a Green Card. This temporary policy rider gives you the same coverage as you have at home.

WHEN THINGS GO WRONG

Reporting
Report all thefts, assaults and traffic accidents to the local police immediately.
In addition, and as soon as possible, report the loss or theft of:

● Credit cards to the issuing companies (see also pp. 96-7).
● Your personal chequebook and/or cheque guarantee card to your bank.
● Travellers' cheques to the nearest office of the issuing company and furnish them with the list of relevant serial numbers.

INSURANCE

Premiums are determined by several factors.

● The duration of travel, with a maximum of three months in one year.
● The size of car engine.
● The type of domestic cover you have.
● Where you go; there is one rate for all of Western Europe, and a higher rate for Eastern Bloc countries and Morocco.
● The age of all named drivers, a higher rate being charged for drivers under 21.

You can also get a bail bond, which guarantees your legal costs up to a specified limit. This is recommended if you are planning to drive in Spain, where you can be arrested for any motoring offence.

Motoring organizations offer special insurance to cover the costs associated with a breakdown, such as garage labour and spare parts, hotel accommodation and alternative transport.

You can also get insurance coverage for hiring cars abroad.

REMEMBER!
● *The best insurance is to take care of yourself and your property as if you were uninsured.*
● *Keep receipts as proof of purchase and value of missing items.*
● *Always try to get a police report in cases of theft. In some countries police may be reluctant to issue a report unless violence has occurred.*
● *Get the tour operator's report if an incident occurs while you are part of an organized tour party.*
● *Keep your record of travellers' cheques serial numbers separate from the cheques.*

● Your passport to the nearest embassy or consulate to arrange for a temporary replacement.

Making a claim
Insurers ask you for as much of the following documentation as possible in support of your claim:
● Completed claim form.
● Original certificate of insurance.
● Tour operator's confirmation of booking or tickets.
● Receipts for all items claimed.

● Name, address and policy number of your household insurance.
● Police report, if claiming for lost money.
● Property Irregularity Report completed in your presence by the air, shipping, coach or rail carrier to whom you must report the loss or damage when it occurs.

PERSONAL SAFETY

PERSONAL SAFETY

The fear of robbery and assault is, for many people, much greater than the real risks they face. Their perception of potential danger may be influenced by dramatic crime reports. Equally, statistics cited in newspapers and on radio and television news programmes, which are often quoted out of context, can be misleading and frightening. Fear is not a useful weapon in self-defence; awareness is.

THE TRUTH ABOUT CRIME

In evaluating the accuracy of any story you should always consider the source of the report and the motivation behind it. For example, a manufacturer of security products might emphasize the rise in the number of reported burglaries to promote his products; a politician might call attention to increased crime rates to support his position on law and order issues; a newspaper might highlight particular incidents in a sensational way in order to sell more papers.

It is also important to realize that a rise in *reported* crimes does not necessarily mean that crime is increasing. Rather, it may indicate that more victims or witnesses are notifying the police, which improves the chances of apprehending the criminals.

MINIMIZING THE RISKS

Most crimes that affect your personal safety are preventable, and most thefts of or from wallets and handbags are avoidable. Like burglary, crimes against the person are often opportunistic; the criminal is looking for an easy target.

Awareness
At home you can protect yourself by using locks and alarms; when you are out and about your best defence is to avoid putting yourself in a dangerous situation. In order to do that, you must be aware of where the dangers lie. It is largely a matter of common sense.

For example, consider the areas you frequent in your home, work and social life. Rural and affluent suburban areas are clearly less risky than troubled inner city areas and depressed housing estates. Busy urban centres are unlikely settings for assault, but provide rich pickings for pickpockets and bag-snatchers.

If you are out late at night, or in the very early hours of the morning, you are more at risk if you walk through parks, commons and subways, or are dependent on infrequent public transport, than if you travel by private transport. Always plan how you will get home; don't rely on chance lifts from friends and never accept a lift from a stranger.

A confident appearance
The message you broadcast by the way in which you walk and behave has a significant influence on whether you are chosen as a target. A criminal is more likely to pick on you if you seem to be frightened, than if you radiate an air of self-confidence.

Intuition

Always trust your feelings. Many victims of crime have revealed that they anticipated the attack on an instinctive level, but didn't take evasive action because there were no overt or concrete signals to confirm their suspicions. Follow your instincts: it is better to be safe than sorry.

CRIME FACTS

Don't impair the quality of your life by worrying needlessly. The truth about attacks is:

- According to the British Crime Survey, only 5 per cent of crimes are violent.

- Most common assaults cause little or no injury.

- The majority of assault victims are men in their 20s who have committed assault themselves.

- Relatively few pensioners are victims of attack, although such incidents are widely reported.

- Nearly half the victims of crimes of violence – wounding, robbery and sexual offences – know their attacker.

REMEMBER!

- *Don't be afraid – be aware.*
- *Act on your instincts.*
- *Don't take unnecessary risks.*
- *Unprovoked attacks on innocent people are rare.*

SELF-DEFENCE and the LAW

In the unfortunate event that you are attacked, your main aim is to escape. You probably won't have any time to think about what the law allows you to do in your own defence. Women, in particular, are often advised to muster all their strength and use the greatest force they can to defend themselves. But the law exists to protect everyone, even your assailant, and you should know when your act of self-defence might be considered an offence.

REASONABLE FORCE

The Criminal Law Act (1967) allows you to use 'reasonable force' to defend yourself. This means as much force as necessary to prevent the attack from continuing and to permit you to escape at the earliest opportunity.

If you injure or kill your attacker, the court will decide whether or not you used reasonable force in trying to defend yourself. This is a subjective and arbitrary area of the law, with no hard and fast rules. Each case is judged on its own merits. However, rulings against male victims are rare, and rulings against female victims are virtually unheard of.

First strike capability
The law does permit you to strike first in self-defence if you should feel sufficiently menaced. For example, if you are convinced that your attacker is going to hit you, you don't have to wait to be hit before defending yourself. You may also strike first to defend another person in the same circumstances.

However, you may never strike vindictively to get revenge after the immediate danger to yourself or another person has passed. For example, if you think that your assailant is about to grab you, you may kick him in the shins. However, while he is grasping his leg in agony, you may not hit him over the head with your umbrella: your primary responsibility is to escape.

WEAPONS
Offensive weapons
An offensive weapon is a knife, gun, or any object adapted for the purpose of causing injury, such as a sharpened metal comb for stabbing or a container of ground pepper for throwing in the eyes.

You are forbidden by law to carry an offensive weapon for any reason, including self-defence. This means you are breaking the law simply by having such a weapon with you in a public place, even if you do not use it.

One reason the law forbids carrying offensive weapons is to protect you. An attacker might easily take the weapon from you and then use it against you.

Gun law
You may legally acquire, keep and use a firearm – a rifle, pistol, revolver, shotgun, and some air weapons – only if you first get a firearms certificate from the police.

The Firearms Acts of 1968 and 1982 specify the regulations governing the possession and use of each type of firearm.

You may not use any firearm for self-defence in any circumstances. Even finding an intruder in your home does not justify you in threatening him with a loaded gun, let alone firing at him.

Store a firearm unloaded and in a separate place from its ammunition. Keep both under lock and key and absolutely inaccessible to children.

Keep hand guns for sport locked up at the club where you practise.

Permitted weapons

To defend yourself, you may use any object that you normally carry, such as an umbrella, a pen or pencil, a perfume or breath spray or a set of keys – assuming, of course, that you can reach them in time.

● Keys held so that they protrude from between your fingers at knuckle level can make a formidable metal 'claw'. This can be done most effectively using a rod-style keyholder.

● Any kind of personal or domestic spray, such as scent, deodorant, breath freshener or insect repellent, aimed straight into an attacker's face may gain you vital seconds for escape.

Commercial aerosol mace sprays and similar products are illegal.

● A closed compact umbrella can be used to wind an attacker. Hold it firmly in both hands at hip level and give a sharp, straight, bayonet-style forward thrust.

A long umbrella can be used to strike low at the assailant's legs; if you wave it higher, aiming at his head, for example, he could easily snatch it from you.

SELF-DEFENCE and the LAW

REMEMBER!

● *Your first responsibility is to escape.*

● *Any offensive weapon you have can be seized by a criminal and used against you.*

● *You may use reasonable force to defend yourself or another person.*

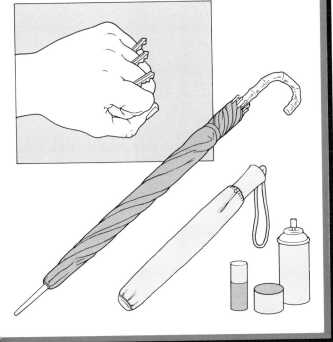

SELF-DEFENCE TRAINING

One of the greatest values of self-defence training is that it enhances your awareness and self-confidence, and thus makes you a less likely target. But you can't learn effective self-defence from a book.

If you want to learn how to defend yourself, ask about courses at your local sports or community centre, adult education institute or martial arts school. The types of courses that are available are outlined below.

Metropolitan police 'Specials' (the

The distinction between self-defence and the various martial arts devoted to unarmed combat is often hazy.

THE MARTIAL ARTS

Any of the Asian-originated martial arts, practised properly, is nothing less than a way of life. Each combines related mental, physical and spiritual disciplines. To be trained effectively in martial arts requires a commitment comparable to that made by a concert musician or an Olympic athlete.

What has always captured the Western imagination is the way in which the attacker's strength and aggression can be turned against him. This is achieved through a flow of evasive and defensive movements, and the judicious application of leverage.

Evasive movements
These train you to:
1 Keep your balance, usually by adopting a widened stance with a low centre of gravity.
● Meet your attacker sideways on so that you reduce his intended target area.
● Pivot correctly.

Defensive movements
These are made in response to an attack, but can also pre-empt the attacker's first strike.

A movement is often toward, rather than away from, the attacker. This not only confuses your assailant, but robs him of his power.

Defensive movements may be grouped as follows:
2 Locks, holds and use of pressure points stop and immobilize the attacker.
3 Trips, throws, sweeps and pushes unbalance the attacker.
4 Strikes with hand and foot disable the attacker.

THE DIFFERENT SCHOOLS
Each martial art tends to emphasize either strikes or locks and throws, the latter being more purely defensive.

Aikido
● Japanese origin.
● Accentuates locks and throws, controlled leverage and use of pressure points.
● Armed variations with wooden swords and rubber knives are also taught.

Judo
● A Japanese-Chinese hybrid, evolved from the more ancient jiu jitsu, which uses a higher proportion of strikes.
● Emphasizes trips and throws, many of which rely on gripping the opponent's clothing.
● Widely practised as a sport from club to Olympic level.

volunteer Special Forces) sometimes offer courses to groups who can organize themselves and provide their own premises. They may also arrange talks and demonstrations.

SELF-DEFENCE TRAINING

Karate
● Of Okinawan, Chinese and Japanese descent.
● The premiere striking art. Despite the popular image of the blade-hand chopping wood, it is high kicks and power punches that predominate.

Kung Fu
● The umbrella title for more than 200 Chinese martial arts, encompassing every variation of style from the staccato, block-and-strike Wing Chung to the lyrical sweeps and pushes of Tai Chi.
● Check what is being taught if a course is described simply as Kung Fu.

Taekwondo
● Korean origin.
● Emphasizes strikes in general and the high kick in particular.
● Showy and spectacular, but probably too ambitious for practical amateur self-defence.

SELF-DEFENCE

Most people don't have several hours a day to devote to studying a martial art and acquiring skills they might never need to use. By contrast, self-defence is a looser discipline involving a collection of physical techniques, many of which are borrowed or adapted from the various martial arts.

The drawbacks
Although basic training in self-defence can be beneficial in raising your level of awareness and confidence, there is no guarantee you will be able to apply it in the event of a real attack.

Classroom training can't always prepare you for the effects of darkness or the element of surprise and the sheer speed with which an attack might occur.

In a real attack you don't have time to review the theory and select the appropriate response. If what you have learned is any less ingrained than a reflex action, it may not help you.

Choosing a course
Attend a short, general self-defence course run by a recognized group or the local police.

Then, if you decide you want to study a classic Oriental martial art, ask if you can observe sessions of different courses so that you can find the one that interests you most.

REMEMBER!
● *In the event of an attack, your primary goal is to escape.*
● *Self-defence training is not a substitute for taking common-sense precautions.*
● *No matter what your skills, don't take risks.*

SAFETY BEGINS at HOME

You should always follow the procedures the police call the 'doorstep code' before you allow a stranger to enter your home. Anyone who calls on you uninvited owes you a sound explanation for being there.

You are under no obligation to admit him or her if you don't want to, and you don't have to give a reason.

Most callers are on legitimate business – performing services, selling, canvassing or

THE DOORSTEP CODE

● Install an outside light above the front door so that you can see callers clearly after dark (see pp. 26-7, and Arriving Home, right).
● Use a door viewer and ask the caller's name *every* time you answer the door (see pp. 30-1).
  Don't open the door until you are sure who is there and that you want to see him or her.
● If the caller is a stranger, always use a door chain or limiter when you open the door.
● If the caller claims to be an official – public service employee, postman, or even the police – open the door with the chain in place and ask for proof of identity.
  Take your time examining any document and satisfy yourself that it is genuine (see pp. 32-3).
● If you are in any doubt, ask the person either to wait or to come back later so that you can ring the company he or she

claims to represent for verification.
● If the caller is abusive or in any way suspect, ring 999 immediately and inform the police. Give the most detailed description of the caller that you can.
● If a stranger asks to use your telephone in an emergency, offer to make the call yourself while he waits outside.
● If you think that someone is trying to break into your home at any time, ring the police.
● Don't place advertisements in the newspaper or local shop window that would result in people calling at your home when you might be there alone.
● If you are trying to sell or rent your home, don't show prospective buyers or tenants around on your own.
  Insist that an estate agent's representative accompanies them, or ask a friend or neighbour to join you.

Arriving home

● Have your doorkeys out and ready to use.
● Have a light on outside when you return home after dark (see pp. 26-7).
● Keep garden plants trimmed so that they can't conceal an intruder.
● As you approach your door, have a good look in all directions before putting your key in the lock. Let yourself in promptly and lock the door behind you.
● If there are signs of intrusion, don't go in (see pp. 64-5).

Taking care with keys (see pp. 28-9)

● Never hide keys outside.
● Avoid lending keys to workmen.
● Don't leave spare keys with the building porter unless you want to; you are not obligated to do so.
● Change the locks when you move into a new home.
● Replace the locks immediately if the keys to your home are lost or stolen.
● If you habitually lock yourself out, keep a spare, unmarked set of keys in a safe place at work or with a trusted neighbour.

WOMEN LIVING ALONE

● Don't put your title (Miss/Mrs/Ms) or your first name on the doorbell or letterbox.
● Avoid any indication that your home is empty during the day, to discourage an attacker who might break in to lie in wait.
● Always close the curtains or blinds when you are home after dark.
● If you use an outside line to dry your clothes, consider hanging up some men's clothing too.
● When you go to answer the door, call out 'I'll go' loudly enough for the person outside to assume someone else is in the home.

seeking your opinion – and will not be offended by your sensible security precautions. Make sure that you and everyone in your household follows the guidelines below at all times.

SAFETY BEGINS at HOME

THE ELDERLY
If you are elderly, there are some points about your personal security to which you probably need to give greater attention than when you were younger.
● Check the condition of door and window frames in property that has been continuously occupied for many years.
    Council grants may be available to repair or improve rotten frames.
● You may also be able to get financial aid to buy and fit security hardware, including door viewers, chains and locks.
● If you suffer from poor eyesight, or stiff or shaking hands, you can choose special locks with large keys and simple latches, doorplates with hand rests, and easy-to-use chains that loop over the door handle.
● You are a preferred target for bogus callers (see pp. 32-3). *Always* apply the 'doorstep code' (see left).
● Have a private code of knocks or rings for regular callers.
● Don't hoard cash; keep it in a bank or other savings institution.

● Keep other valuables in a bank or have a wall safe installed (see pp. 60-1).
● If you are worried about intruders, have a panic button alarm installed by the front door and in your bedroom (see pp. 54-5).
    There are also alarms that sound if a would-be intruder tampers with the door handle.
● If possible, have a telephone by your bedside.

In an emergency
● If you hear an intruder enter your home at night, dial 999 from your bedside telephone or push your panic alarm button.
● If you don't have a telephone or an alarm, turn on the light and make a loud noise.
● Don't go out of your room to confront the intruder.
    If possible, keep a watch through the window so you can see what he looks like and the direction in which he runs off.

Neighbourhood involvement
● Join your Neighbourhood Watch (see pp. 146-9). People who are at

home during the day, when most burglaries occur, are of particular value.
● Find out about working with your local Victims Support Scheme.
● Take advantage of security advice and information offered by Age Concern and Help the Aged.
    They can tell you if you qualify for grants to improve your security.
● Let your neighbours know if you have an audible alarm system, so they will respond quickly if they hear it.

Cold and the old
If you have elderly relatives, friends or neighbours:
● Make sure that they have sufficient heating and hot food in cold weather.
● Review the fire prevention precautions in their homes (see pp. 66-7).
● Suggest they wear a wristwatch-style temperature monitor that sends a radio signal alarm if their body temperature drops too low.
● Suggest they install a special thermostat that sets off an alarm if the room temperature becomes too low.

REMEMBER!
● *Your personal safety is your top priority.*
● *Always follow the 'doorstep code'.*
● *Review your level of household security (see pp. 12-77).*
● *Ring the police if you have a suspicious caller or hear someone trying to break into your home.*

CHILDREN'S SAFETY

Children are particularly vulnerable to crime because of their size and limited experience. Not only can their bicycles be stolen or their pocket money extorted by bullying peers, but they may be physically as well as psychologically at risk from adults who molest children.

Parents, teachers and other adults who work with children must protect them by teaching them sensible and responsible patterns of behaviour without inducing morbid pessimism. Children need to be

ADEQUATE SUPERVISION

How much independence you allow children, and how much supervision you think they need, will depend partly on their maturity and partly on the area in which you live. Inner cities are generally more risky than rural areas, but even affluent suburbs can pose dangers.

● Never leave small children alone at home, in a car, playing in the street or in any public place. A child regularly left alone is vulnerable not only to danger from other people, but also to accidents and fear.

● Always see small children safely to and from school. Organize a rota with other parents and be sure you always know the person taking responsibility for your child.

● Don't send small children on errands unaccompanied, no matter how near home.

● A child who owns and can ride a bicycle will be venturing out. Don't give a bike to a child until he or she has learnt to tell the time, use the telephone, communicate freely and generally behave responsibly.

Stranger danger

Before you allow children to go out of the home alone, even to play in the front garden, make sure they understand how to treat a stranger.

● *A stranger is anyone you don't know, even if they seem to know you.* Tell children to try to remember details about the clothing, appearance or car of any stranger who approaches them.

● *Don't talk to a stranger.* Make sure that children know when they should disobey an adult. Explain that by disregarding the attentions or orders of a stranger, they are obeying you.

● *Never go anywhere with a stranger.* Give children examples of the kinds of tricks a stranger might use. Ask them what they would do, for example, if a stranger offered them sweets, a ride in a car, money, toys, or a chance to play with a kitten or puppy. Explain that these bribes are a way of trying to make them do something wrong; they are not presents.

● *Shout 'No' or 'I don't know him/her' as loud as you can if a stranger tries to touch you.* It is all right to do anything – kick, bite, scratch, scream – to escape from a stranger.

Out and about

Don't let your children go out alone until they know:

● There is safety in numbers; they should keep in a group or with at least one other child.

● They can always approach a uniformed police officer if they need help or want to report suspicious behaviour.

● Their full name, address and telephone number; it is a good idea to know a neighbour's name and telephone number too.

● How to use a public telephone to call you at home or at work, and how to reverse the charges if they don't have any money.

● How to dial 999 in an emergency.

aware, not frightened. Talking to your children, and making sure they feel they can always talk to you, are among the greatest securities you can give them.

CHILDREN'S SAFETY

● They mustn't play in dark or deserted areas, on rubbish tips or railway lines, or in derelict buildings.

● They must always let you know where they are going. Make sure you know how they are getting there and back. Tell them what time to be home and make sure they stick to it.

DON'T TOUCH ME

Most sexual offences against children are committed by people they know, usually relatives. Make sure your children know:

● They should not let *anyone* touch them in a manner they find objectionable.

● The difference between acceptable shows of affection and inappropriate physical contact.

● The difference between good secrets and bad secrets. They should tell you if an older person has asked them to keep any contact between them a secret.

● They must always ask your permission before they accept any treat or present, or an invitation to go anywhere, even to a neighbour's home.

● They should tell you immediately if they have been offered bribes, even if they don't accept them. Always ask how they acquired any items you can't account for.

If something happens

Your child should always tell you if someone has tried to touch him or her.

If your child claims to have been sexually abused or assaulted:

● Always believe him or her. Children rarely invent such incidents and are more likely to conceal them.

● Reassure the child that you will protect him or her from the offender.

● Reassure the child that he or she is not to blame. The worst damage occurs when children transfer the offender's guilt to themselves.

● If the child is having trouble describing the incident, let him or her use a doll or teddy bear to show what happened.

● Ring the police immediatley and report the incident.

REMEMBER!

● *If your child is missing, call the police at the earliest opportunity. A false alarm is always preferable to an avoidable tragedy.*

● *Shirts or jackets emblazoned with your child's first name give strangers an unfair means of familiarity.*

● *A child's greatest defence is awareness and full communication with you.*

● *Children virtually never invent stories of sexual interference: always believe them.*

WOMEN OUT and ABOUT

Street crime is as opportunistic as burglary. In the same way that you protect your home, you can protect yourself by minimizing the criminal's opportunities.

You don't need to take all the precautions listed here all the time. Use your common sense to judge situations in which you are generally safe, and those in which your risks are greater, and act accordingly. For example, the chances of having your handbag snatched are greater in a crowded shopping area than on a

PERSONAL VALUABLES

In all situations
● Carry your bank card separately from your cheque book.
● An open handbag or basket is an invitation to trouble.

A bag carried by a hand-held strap can easily be snatched.

A bag with a flap and secure fastener, carried in your hand, is the most secure.

Clasp one end of the bag in the palm of your hand, and tuck the other end in your elbow joint, with the flap toward you.

● Hold a shoulder bag with the strap forward and the flap toward your body (see pp. 100-1).
● Avoid carrying items you know you don't need that day, such as your savings passbook, cheque book, excess cash, other identification, including correspondence.

In high-risk situations
● Carry your purse in a secure pocket in your clothing, not in your handbag.
● Carry your housekeys securely

on your person. Then if your bag is lost or stolen, you will not be locked out and you will not need to get your locks changed (see pp. 28-9).
● Conceal or avoid wearing expensive looking jewellery, especially around the neck.

WALK THIS WAY

In all situations
● Look confident and purposeful. Keep your head and eyes up, shoulders back, stride steadily.
● Stay alert. Keep looking and listening.

● Don't take shortcuts along unlit or deserted roads, through subways or across parks and commons. Choose the long way round via well-lit main roads.
● Face oncoming traffic to reduce the risk of kerb-crawlers.
● Write down a kerb-crawler's vehicle registration number and report it to the police.
● Have your housekeys ready to let yourself in without delay or fumbling.
● If you think you are being followed, cross the road and walk on

PERSONAL ALARMS

In high-risk situations
● Carry a shrill or shriek alarm in your pocket.

A gas-powered alarm is lighter, smaller and easier to carry than a battery-powered model. However, it sounds only while you press it, and it can run out of fuel unexpectedly.

A battery-powered alarm continues to sound once activated, even if you drop it. You can check to see if the battery needs replacing.

● Don't wear an alarm around your neck; it could be used to choke you.
● Carry a security briefcase with a built-in alarm, which sounds if the case is snatched.

TRAVELLING ALONE AT NIGHT
There is real safety in numbers: it is very rare for two or more people to be attacked. However, if you must travel alone, observe the following rules

In all situations
● Make plans for getting home safely

before you go out.
● Avoid deserted bus stops; go to a more populated area.
● Never accept a lift from a stranger, even if he claims to be a private taxi.
● On trains, sit in compartments with other people, or near the guard.
● If you are threatened with an attack on a train, move to another compartment or carriage.

If that is not possible, pull the emergency cord. Do not pull the cord between stations

unless you have no alternative.
● If you have been driven home, ask the driver to wait until you are safely indoors.
● Don't drink too much; it impairs your judgement and makes you more vulnerable.
● Do not hitchhike.

In high-risk situations
● Have money for a taxi and the telephone number of a reputable taxi company.
● Sit downstairs on doubledecker buses, as near the driver or other women as possible.

suburban residential street; the risk of being assaulted is greater after dark in a deserted area than during the day or on a well-lit and busy street.

Be aware and be careful, but don't worry unnecessarily.

WOMEN OUT and ABOUT

the other side.

If you are still being followed, head for a busy public place, such as a pub, or fire or police station.

If you are in a residential area, go toward the nearest well-lit house. Most followers will not wait around to see if you are let in.

Try not to lead the person to your own car or home.

Ring the police at the first opportunity.

In high-risk situations
● Don't walk home alone after dark.

● Walk down the middle of the pavement, rather than near shrubbery or dark doorways where a criminal may be lurking.
● As you walk, look for places where an attacker might be hiding, and for escape routes.
● Wear sensible shoes. Although a stiletto heel has its uses in self-defence, flight is always preferable to a fight, and in the latter keeping your balance is crucial.
● If a group of potential

troublemakers is loitering in your path, cross the road before you near them.

Don't respond to any comments. Appear unimpressed and keep walking.
● Keep your hands out of your pockets, unless you are holding a shrill alarm; you might need them free to defend yourself.
● Avoid eye contact with strangers; it may be interpreted as provocative.
● A personal stereo can be a liability, since it decreases your awareness of sounds around you.

REMEMBER!
● *Don't worry needlessly.*
● *Always plan ahead.*
● *There is safety in numbers.*

● Sit near the door on a bus or train only if it is near the driver or guard. Bag-snatchers want a quick exit and will head for unguarded doors.
● If you regularly work late, vary your route home to avoid attracting attention as an easy target.
● Let someone know where you are going and how and when you expect to arrive, so that the alarm can be raised if you fail to turn up.

IN PUBLIC PLACES
● At cash points, look in both directions

before and after using your card. Put the cash away quickly.
● At a public telephone, don't rest your handbag on the ledge or clutch it between your feet.

Keep your wrist or shoulder through the strap and stand at an angle to the street with your bag inward.
● In supermarkets, don't leave your handbag unguarded in your basket or trolley.
● In shops and stores, don't leave your bag unattended on a chair, the floor, or in a changing room.

SPECIAL TIPS FOR THE ELDERLY
● A special shrill alarm can be attached to a walking stick or clothing. It sounds if the stick or the person lies flat for more than a few moments.
● Vary the time and day on which you collect your pension.
● Ask your local Crime Prevention Officer, Help the Aged or Age Concern Office about special talks on self-defence for your age group.

IN the CAR

Crimes involving vehicles with the driver present are comparatively unusual, but they do occur. The criminal's target may be your car, your personal property, or even you. As with other types of crime, you can minimize your risks by reducing the criminal's opportunities. Think of your car as your home on wheels, and show the same regard for your security while you are driving as you would at home.

WOMEN ALONE

● On long trips or when travelling after dark, let family or friends at both ends of your journey know your departure time, your route and expected arrival time. Ring to say you have arrived safely.

● Plan your route in advance. Carry the relevant maps to avoid having to stop and ask directions.

● Before you travel, make sure your car is in good working order and check that it has enough oil, water and petrol.

● Carry change and a phonecard for a public telephone.

● If your car breaks down while you are travelling at night and you don't know how to fix it, ring the breakdown service from a public or emergency telephone.

If you are not near a telephone, lock yourself in the car and wait for help from the police or those who are expecting you to arrive.

● If you leave your car to get help, do not accept lifts from a man on his own or with other men. Use your common sense in deciding whether to accept a lift from a woman or a man and a woman together.

● Try to avoid travelling alone after dark, particularly on back lanes in rural areas. If you can't avoid it, carry a pocket torch in case you have to get out of the car.

● Do not leave your handbag lying on the front or back passenger seat; put it on the floor out of sight.

● Carry a pocket alarm as an added precaution for use when you enter and leave the car after dark.

● Unless you are a witness, do not stop where a car appears to have had an accident or broken down: it could be a trap. Drive on to the next telephone or police station and report it.

● Don't pick up hitchhikers if you are alone, no matter how helpless they look.

● A car telephone enhances your security if you frequently travel long distances alone and at night. It enables you to call for help from the safety of your vehicle if the car breaks down, and to notify people if you are delayed or in trouble.

If you are followed

● Do not let yourself be forced off the road.

● Memorize the following vehicle's registration number.

● Try to alert other motorists by flashing your lights and sounding your horn.

● Keep driving until you reach any busy public place, or a police, fire or open petrol station.

● Avoid leading a following vehicle into your own driveway if possible.

● If you are followed into your own or another driveway, stay locked in your car and sound your horn and flash your lights to attract attention. This in itself will probably frighten away your pursuer.

PARKING

● In general, always park in a busy, well-lit street. Your vehicle is less likely to be attacked and you will feel more secure leaving and returning to it.

● Multi-storey car parks can be dangerous. They tend to be poorly lit and provide a thief or assailant with opportunities to hide and surprise you, and to escape.

If you must use one, park as near as you can to the entrance/exit.

● When you are travelling alone and stop to use motorway services, park as near the main building as possible.

IN the CAR

Getting into your car

● Have your keys out and ready to use.
● Before you unlock the door, quickly check the back seat to make sure that no one has got in. Use a pocket torch after dark.
● If you drive through areas you don't know, or know or suspect to be unsafe, lock your doors and keep your windows high enough to prevent anyone reaching in.

ABDUCTION AND HIJACKING

These crimes are unlikely to affect most drivers, but they are a cause of concern to people who transport valuable goods, and to some executives.

There are two security devices to protect potential victims.
● A hijack victim might be saved by a simulated mechanical breakdown. When the hidden switch is thrown, the fuel line is interrupted.

The car can be restarted only with a second switch sited elsewhere in the vehicle.
● Drivers with a special two-way relay car telephone linked to a chain of receiving stations can report suspicious behaviour or attempted attacks.

Pre-programmed cell-phones will dial through at the touch of a single button.

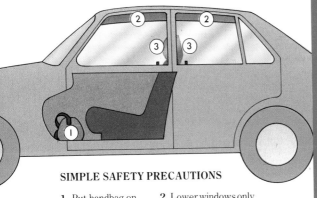

SIMPLE SAFETY PRECAUTIONS

1 Put handbag on the floor, not on the passenger seat.

2 Lower windows only a short way.
3 Keep all doors locked.

REMEMBER!

● *Keep your car doors locked and windows high enough to prevent someone reaching inside.*
● *Always park in the best-lit area available.*
● *If alone, don't stop if you see a breakdown. Instead, drive on and report it later.*
● *Be aware of vehicle security precautions (see pp. 78-95).*

IF YOU ARE ATTACKED

If you take the sensible precautions advised throughout this book, you will minimize your chances of being the victim of any crime. It is also sensible to know how to react in the event of an attack, so that you can escape quickly and unharmed.

In the event of any attack, you should:
1 Activate your alarm.
2 Shout, even if there doesn't appear to be anyone around to hear you.
3 Look for an escape.

BAG-SNATCH

Women are the main targets of bag-snatchers, but men carrying briefcases or over-the-shoulder camera cases are also vulnerable.
● Most bag-snatchers attack on the run, using a 'forward grab' manoeuvre.
If they don't succeed, many just keep running, so always hold your bag firmly.
● Never pursue a thief unless you are in no doubt that you can overpower him.
● If a struggle develops or is threatened, surrender your bag: your safety comes first.

ASSAULT

If someone attacks you or threatens to:
● Try to stay calm: it improves your chances of getting away quickly.
● Observe as much detail about him as you can.
● Shout or scream to attract attention and to startle the attacker.
● Enhance your balance by taking a wider stance and bending your knees.
● If your attacker is armed, use your bag as a shield or to dislodge the weapon.

● If your attacker is unarmed, you are better off with empty hands.
Throw your bag or case at him or into the middle of the road behind you.
● Look for the area on the attacker's body where you can most easily land a hard blow (see pp. 126-7).
Although you might think a sharp poke in the eyes is the most disabling blow, if you are too short to reach effectively, you are better off giving a sharp kick in the shins.
Retain the element of surprise; don't make preparatory movements or stare directly at the target before striking – just a quick glance to orient yourself.
● If the attacker pulls you, move *with*, rather than away from, him. This gives you a better chance of getting him off balance.
● If you use your fist, remember to fold the thumb outside, not inside, your fingers or you could hurt your hand.
● Put all the force you can into your first strike; if it fails, try another, but always run at the first chance you get.

Attackers with knives

● Always be aware of where the weapon is.
● Don't make any sudden moves.
● Try to assess the attacker's intentions, but don't oppose him immediately.
● If you can distract him, or if some outside occurence distracts him, try to knock the weapon out of his hand, then RUN!
● Use anything you are holding or can reach as a shield to avoid direct contact with the knife.

In your home

● Don't run into the bedroom or bathroom and lock yourself in; do run into the street.
● Try not to leave knives or scissors lying out; better to keep a rolling pin in reach in the kitchen.

Bedside panic button

Attackers with guns

● There is no defence against a gun. There is no practical manoeuvre for escaping from, or overpowering, an armed assailant.
● Stay as calm as possible and observe all the detail you can.
● Do as you are told.
● Try to reason with your attacker; keep talking, but avoid being provocative.

● If you hear an intruder when you are in bed, try to escape without turning on the light. You know the layout of your home – he doesn't.
● Use your panic button alarm (see pp. 54-5) if you have one.

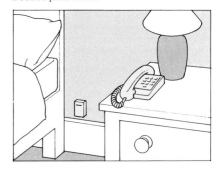

IF YOU ARE ATTACKED

Raise knee Snap kick Resume stance

TIPS FOR TOES
● If you use your feet in self-defence, flex your toes backward as you kick. If you kick with your toes pointed you could injure your foot.
● The snap-kick makes you less vulnerable to having your foot grabbed and being thrown off balance.
 Raise the knee of your kicking leg first, then quickly snap the foot out and back.

CONTINUITY
One of the most valuable principles of martial arts training, which can be applied to any form of self-defence, is a continuous movement that begins and ends with a stable, balanced posture.

● A kick does not end the moment your foot strikes the attacker's body, but when your foot is back on the ground.
● Aim a blow *through*, not at, the attacker's body.
● To be effective, a throw must be performed as a single, unbroken movement.

REMEMBER!
● *Your main goal is to escape.*
● *Surrender any valuables rather than risk your physical safety.*
● *If you fight, aim for the body target you can reach most easily.*
● *Always put your full power into your first strike.*
● *Test yourself now to see how you would react to a physical attack.*

BE PREPARED
● Test yourself now. Ask a friend to tackle you, so that you can find out what your natural reactions are.
 Many people find that even when they know an attack is coming and is not in earnest, they simply crumple up and wait for it to stop.

If this is your reaction, you would benefit from proper self-defence training.
● The following pages illustrate basic principles common to most self-defence training.
 Act them out with a partner, just to get the feeling of the movements involved.

To learn how to use them effectively, attend a course run by a qualified self-defence instructor.
● Review the precautions and procedures in this chapter frequently; even a mental rehearsal can be helpful.

BODY WEAPONS and TARGETS

Even if you have not studied any of the techniques of self-defence, you can use the arsenal of natural 'weapons' in *your* body to protect yourself. These weapons and the ways they can be used are shown below.

Your attacker is vulnerable too. You should aim for those areas on *his* body to which you can do the most damage with a single blow, since your object is to disable him, even momentarily, so that you can

BODY WEAPONS

Fingers
1 Eye poke.
● Throat jab.
● Twisting attacker's fingers.
● Scratching.
● Squeezing.

Hands
● Punching.
● Pushing.

Elbows
These are the hardest parts of the body.
2 Sharp backward or sideways blows.

Hips and buttocks
● Slamming and unbalancing.

Knees
3 Sharp upward blows.

Skull
● Headbutting.

Teeth
4 Biting.

Feet
5 Kicking.
● Scraping.
● Stamping.

Voice
● Raising an alarm.
● Intimidating: a shout is the vocal equivalent of a punch!
● Raising your adrenalin and focusing the power of any blow you deliver.

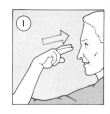
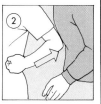
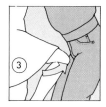
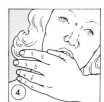

BODY TARGETS

The target you attack will be determined by the areas you can reach (see also pp. 128-33).
● Do not bother trying to strike or punch an attacker on the chest or arms – it will have no effect.
● Concentrate all your efforts on trying to unbalance, surprise, disorientate or hurt your attacker so that you can RUN!
● Shout and strike simultaneously to increase the shock to your attacker and to give yourself courage.
● If you cannot act aggressively for your own sake, imagine you are defending someone you love.

1 Hair
● Pull hard.
● Grasp and use to smash head into any available hard surface.

2 Ears
● Clap hard with your hands firmly cupped.

3 Face
● Scratch hard with fingernails.

4 Eyes
Don't even attempt these defences unless you are sure you can carry them out with conviction.
● Poke as hard and fast as possible with your forefinger and middle finger stiff and open in a V.
● Poke with any pointed object you have in your pocket.
● Press in with your thumbs.

5 Nose
● Use the heel of your hand to smash upward from underneath.
● Bang hard with your head.

6 Chin
● Use the heel of your hand to smash upward from underneath.

7 Throat
● Strike hard with stiffened fingers, fist or elbow. Aim for the Adam's apple or the hollow just below it.

8 Fingers
● Twist the little fingers backward and apart to break the attacker's hold.

escape. The illustration below illustrates these target areas and outlines the most effective single blows.

BODY WEAPONS and TARGETS

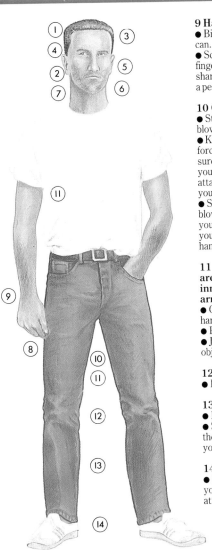

9 Hands
● Bite as hard as you can.
● Scratch with fingernails or any sharp object, such as a pencil, pen, or keys.

10 Groin
● Strike an upward blow with the knee.
● Kick with maximum force *only* if you are sure you will not lose your balance and the attacker cannot grab your foot.
● Strike a forceful blow backward, with your arm straight and your hand in a fist – a hammer-fist blow.

11 Soft, fleshy areas (testicles, inner thigh, inner arm)
● Grasp and twist hard.
● Pinch.
● Jab with sharp object.

12 Knee
● Kick hard.

13 Shin
● Kick hard.
● Scrape down with the heel or edge of your shoe.

14 Feet
● Stamp on hard with your heel if you are attacked from behind.

REMEMBER!
● *Your primary goal is to escape unharmed as soon as possible.*
● *Your personal safety is more important and more valuable than anything in your purse or wallet.*
● *Try to stay calm and breathe regularly.*

ESCAPING ATTACKS from the FRONT

The small advantage of an attack from the front is that you see it coming. You can quickly evaluate your attacker and your situation. You also have the chance to communicate your attitude, which can be a powerful psychological weapon.

● Try to notice as much detail as possible about your attacker so that you can give the police a useful description.

● Try not to let your attacker grab both of

If your arms are held
1 Try to dislodge his arms before his grip is firm: aim for inside the elbows.
2 Summon all your strength to swing your arms forward, up and apart between his arms in one continuous movement, shouting at the same time.
● Follow through and RUN!

If your clothes are grabbed
1 If your arms are free, jab at his throat or eyes hard and fast, shouting at the same time.

2 If your arms are held and you cannot free them, use your head to butt the attacker in the face.
● Follow through and RUN!

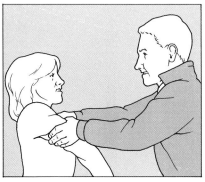

1

1

2

2

your hands at the same time.
● As soon as you have released your attacker's hold on you, follow through with the most effective single blow (see pp. 126-7) to disable him and RUN!

ESCAPING ATTACKS from the FRONT

If he is about to hit you
● Try not to cower or throw your hands up to hide your face.
● Before the blow can land, act *as if you have been* hit. For example, if the attacker seems to be aiming at your head, quickly move your head away from the blow and duck.
   If he aims at your abdomen, drop your head and shoulders down and forward (see pp. 124-5).
● Follow through and RUN!

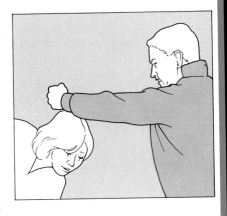

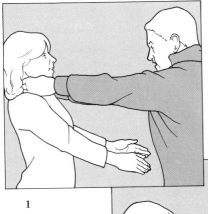

1

If he grabs you around the neck
1 Pull your chin in tightly to reduce the risk of strangulation.
2 Immediately jab your stiffened hand into his throat.
● Then thrust outward with both arms to dislodge his hands.
● Follow through and RUN!

2

REMEMBER!
● *Try not to let your attacker grab both your hands at the same time.*
● *If you are throttled or your clothes are grabbed, your attacker's hands are occupied. This gives you the chance to counter-attack with yours.*
● *Take any action you can as quickly and forcefully as possible.*

129

ESCAPING ATTACKS from BEHIND

An attack from behind takes you by surprise and is difficult to counter, but you can still escape as long as you act both quickly and ferociously.

If choked by an arm around throat
1 Bring your chin down sharply or turn your head sideways to relieve the pressure.
2 Swing your elbow backward with as much force and venom as you can into his stomach or the soft area below his ribs.

3 Dislodge his grip by forcing his little fingers backward or swing a hammer-fist to his groin (see pp. 126-7).
4 Raise your knee and follow through with a backward kick to his shin, and RUN!

1

2

If strangled with hands around your throat
1 Dig your chin in hard and drive a swift hammer-fist backward to his groin.
2 Grasp the assailant's little fingers only (one in each of your hands, ideally before his grip settles), then wrench them backward

quickly with all your strength.
● Then force your arms out sideways at shoulder level, increasing the pressure on his little finger joints.
3, 4 Follow through with a backward kick to the knee, scrape down the shin, and stamp on his foot. And RUN!

1

2

If your arms are held
1 Glance backward quickly to check your target.
2 Kick his knees, scrape his shin and stamp on his instep if you can.
● At the least, stamp hard on his foot.
3 Bite any part of his

hands or arms you can reach.
4 If you are about the same height as your attacker, butt your head back full-force into his face. Shout and kick hard at the same time.
● Follow through with your hardest push and RUN!

1

2

ESCAPING
ATTACKS
from BEHIND

3

4

3

4

3

4

REMEMBER!

● *In any attack from behind, act immediately before you are forced over backward.*

● *Shout loudly and angrily as you strike your attacker.*

● *Try to unbalance your assailant.*

ESCAPING from a GROUND POSITION

Do not give up mentally the moment you are pinned to the ground. You can still unbalance your attacker and use many of the same defence techniques as you would employ in a standing position.

If your attacker is astride you and pinning your wrists to the ground
1 Put all your force into pushing one arm off the ground. This distracts the attacker into shifting his weight to push back.
2 In that instant, shoot your other arm up along the ground above your head.
3 As your attacker shifts his weight up toward your extended arm, roll hard in the same direction and push up with your body and other arm.
4 As soon as you have rolled your attacker off, jump up and RUN!

1

If you are being choked
1 Drive your joined hands – do *not* interlace your fingers – upward to smash his nose. If you can't reach that far, aim for his Adam's apple or the hollow just below it (see pp. 126-7).
2 Immediately draw one leg up with your knee bent so that your foot is flat against the ground.
3 Quickly twist in the opposite direction to roll the attacker off, pulling at his elbow and pushing his wrist to keep his arm locked straight.
4 Follow through with a blow to any target you can reach without the risk of having your leg grabbed, and RUN!

1

If your attacker is in the rape position
1 If he is kneeling between your knees and pinning you down so that you cannot employ either of the above escapes, quickly wrap your legs over his, hooking your feet under his ankles from the inside.
2 Push your legs straight out to the side. This will lock his thighs, pinning him in position.
3 Grab his collar with one hand on either side of his neck.
4 Using the collar for leverage, drive your knuckles hard into his neck just behind his Adam's apple.
This could cause him to black out, allowing you to escape, or at least diminish his hold long enough for you to try another method.

1

If you are forced down with your attacker astride you
1 Pull your chin in hard, and draw your elbows in tight and close to your body.
2 Cup your hands and press them to the ground as a face guard, leaving a triangle-shaped breathing hole for your nose.
3 Use all your strength to round your back by drawing your knees up and elbows together.
4 As soon as you get your back and hips up, roll your attacker onto his back.
● Follow through by striking whatever target you can reach, and RUN!

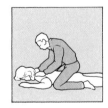

1

ESCAPING from a GROUND POSITION

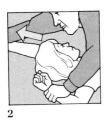
2

3

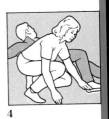
4

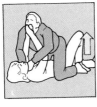
2

3

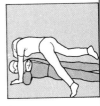
4

REMEMBER!
- *Your first aim is to unbalance your attacker so that you can escape.*

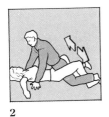
2

3

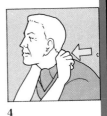
4

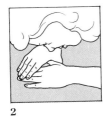
2

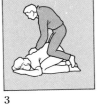
3

4

SEXUAL OFFENCES

Sexual offences include obscene telephone calls, voyeurism, exhibitionism, molesting and rape. There are no harmless sexual offences. Although the victim of an obscene telephone call or a voyeur ('peeping Tom') is not physically injured, it is impossible to quantify the emotional and mental injury she suffers.

In cases of aggressive sexual offences, such as molesting and rape, the physical injuries are compounded by the possibility of disease and pregnancy, harm to existing

PASSIVE OFFENCES

All sexual offences should be reported to the police. Despite the commonly held belief that exhibitionists ('flashers') and voyeurs are harmless, police records show that men convicted of the more aggressive sexual crimes often have a history of these activities.

Obscene calls
● The caller may know you or may have picked your number from the telephone directory or even dialled your number at random.
● Women should never list their first names in the telephone directory.
● Don't talk to an obscene caller. Whether he is a 'heavy breather', asks personal questions or launches into an offensive monologue, just hang up.
● Report persistent callers to British Telecom. You may have to change your number or make it ex-directory.
● If the caller seems to know you are alone and you feel threatened, ring the police.
● Keep a whistle by the telephone. One loud blast down the line will hurt the caller and deter him from calling again.

Voyeurs
● Keep your curtains or blinds drawn after dusk.
● Use external lighting to discourage approach to the house (see pp. 26-7).
● Don't leave all-female laundry on an outside line overnight.
● Report any prowlers to the police, giving as much detail as possible.

Exhibitionists ('flashers')
● If you encounter a man exposing himself, simply walk away. Avoid eye contact and conversation.
● Report the incident to the police immediately, and give as accurate a description of the offender as you can.

Kerb-crawlers
● Walk facing traffic to minimize the risk; if you are moving in the opposite direction, a car can't pursue you.
● Stay far enough away from the road to avoid being grabbed.
● If an incident occurs, memorize the vehicle registration number and report it to the police immediately.

AGGRESSIVE OFFENCES
Molesters ('gropers')
Molesters tend to attack when they are confident their victims can't readily identify them – for example, in very crowded public transport or dark cinemas – or in deserted areas where they think they won't be caught.
● If there are other people around, shout 'Get your hands off me!'; most molesters will slink away mortified.
● If no one is around, escape as soon as you can and inform police immediately.
● If the incident occurs on commercial premises, complain to the management.

relationships and long-term destruction of self-confidence.

Like other criminals, many sexual offenders are opportunists. Your best defence is deterrence and target removal.

SEXUAL ASSAULT AND RAPE

● Follow all the advice for your personal safety given throughout this chapter.
● Avoid deserted pedestrian shortcuts, especially after dark.
● Never accept a lift from a stranger.
● Remember, too much alcohol makes you more vulnerable.
● Be party-wise. Make sure your hosts or friends know any man you meet at a party or public gathering before you agree to leave with him.

If he's a gate-crasher or no one knows him, then he's a stranger – a potential danger. If you want to see him, arrange to meet him in public places until you get to know him.

If the worst happens

In about half the reported cases of sexual assault the victim knows the attacker.

Many more such cases are probably not reported because the victims feel – wrongly – that the attack is, in some way, their fault.

Some women think that because they know the attacker, the authorities will assume that they consented to the attack. This is not true.

● You are urged to report a rape or attempted rape at the earliest opportunity to help the police apprehend the offender.
● If you can, go directly to the nearest police station or ring 999.
● You will be treated sympathetically. Many larger Metropolitan Police stations now have private Victim Examination Suites.

The police will make every effort to have you examined by a woman doctor if that is your preference. They will also contact the local Victims Support Scheme for you (see pp.150-1).

● Remember all the detail you can about your attacker.

Descriptions of tattoos, scars, birthmarks and jewellery are particularly useful in identifying offenders.
● Avoid drinking any alcohol or taking any sort of tranquillizer or drug until you have given your statement.
● Don't bathe or change clothing until you have been examined or you might destroy vital forensic evidence.
● A woman police officer will always be present while you are being interviewed or examined in the police station.
● If you have had serious injuries, the police will get you to hospital immediately.
● You will probably want to see your own doctor to check for sexually transmitted diseases and pregnancy.

The woman police officer will also advise you about post-coital birth control and can arrange for you to receive priority examination at a clinic for sexually transmitted diseases.

SEXUAL OFFENCES

REMEMBER!

● *The more quickly you reach the police, the better their chances of finding your attacker and obtaining a conviction.*
● *Sexual attackers are sometimes deterred by unexpected and off-putting behaviour. It may sound unpleasant, but you might deter a rapist if you make yourself vomit in time.*
● *More than half of the reported incidents of rape occur in the victim's own home.*
● *The Rape Crisis Centre has branches nationwide and offers a 24-hour-a-day service.*

FIRST AID 1

If someone is injured in an accident at home or in a car, or as the result of a street crime, try to get medical help as soon as possible. Ring 999 or ask a passing motorist or pedestrian to do so for you.

Apply the basic principles of first aid shown here and on pages 138-9 to make the injured person as comfortable as possible while you wait for help to arrive. Be careful not to aggravate the victim's

---

CARE OF THE UNCONSCIOUS

RESPIRATION

Check breathing
● Put your ear close to the victim's mouth and nose so that you can hear and feel if air is exhaled.

● Watch and feel his chest to see if it rises and falls.

Clear the airway
If the person is not breathing:
● Turn him gently on his back.
● Clear out the mouth with your fingers.
● Put one hand under his neck and the other on his forehead.

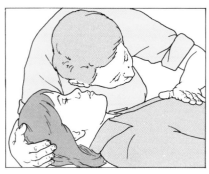 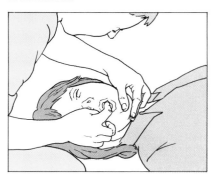

Mouth-to-mouth resuscitation
If the person still is not breathing:
● Pinch his nostrils together.
● Open your mouth

wide and take a normal breath.
● Seal your lips around his mouth.
● Blow into his lungs until you see his chest rise.

● Remove your mouth and wait for his chest to fall.
● Repeat three times very quickly, (making four breaths altogether) and then

at your own normal rate of breathing.
Continue until the victim begins to breathe normally, then place him in the recovery position.

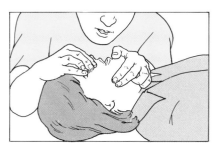 

condition. When a crime is involved, do not tamper with or destroy any forensic evidence.

FIRST AID 1

RECOVERY POSITION

- Lie the victim on his side.
- Place the upper arm near the victim's head with the elbow bent at right angles.

  Let the other arm lie fairly straight, palm upward, just free of the body.
- Bring the upper knee up so that the thigh is also at a right angle to the body.

  Keep the other knee slightly bent.
- *Never* try to give an unconscious person anything to drink.

Gently turn body on to side

Recovery position

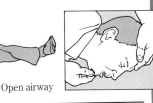

Open airway

REMEMBER!

- *Check that an unconscious victim is breathing.*
- *Tilt head back to open airway.*
- *Do not move anyone who might have fractured bones, especially if spinal injury is suspected.*
- *Get professional medical help as soon as possible.*

SHOCK

A person may go into shock some time after he is injured. He will look pale, and feel faint. He might become drowsy or unconscious, and feel nauseated or begin to vomit.

- Keep him quiet in the recovery position or, if conscious, on his back, with his feet slightly higher than his head.

- Loosen any tight clothing, such as collar, belt or waistband.
- Cover him lightly from chin to toes to prevent heat loss; avoid overwarming him.
- Do not give him any medicine, tablets, food or drink.

FIRST AID 2

Everyone should know the basics of first aid. These are not usually self-administered, but if you are injured and alone, being able to apply some of these techniques to yourself could make a vital difference in an emergency.

EYE INJURIES
Foreign particle
If it is on the pupil or embedded in the eyeball:
● Do not rub.
● Do not attempt to remove.
● Cover the eye lightly with a soft pad or bandage.

If it is under the lid or resting on the surface of the eye:
● Blink.
● Pull the top lid down over the lower lid.

Chemicals
● Quickly flush eye with water for at least 10 minutes.
● Then cover the eye with a light bandage.
● See a doctor.

NOSE BLEED
● Sit up with head slightly forward.
● Pinch the nostrils firmly closed for about 10 minutes and breathe through your mouth.
● Loosen constrictive clothing around the neck.
● Avoid blowing nose.

TREATING WOUNDS

MODERATE BLEEDING
May stop of its own accord. You can:
● Wash the wound with running water, then dry carefully.
● Cover the wound with a clean cloth or dressing and bandage firmly.
● If there is no suspected fracture or spinal injury, lift and support the injured part.

SEVERE BLEEDING
Must be controlled urgently.

Direct pressure
● Use your fingers to apply direct pressure to the bleeding wound.
    Press the sides of a large wound together gently but firmly.
● Lie as comfortably as possible, with head lowered.
● If no fracture is suspected, raise and support the bleeding part.
● Pick out and retain any foreign bodies that can be removed easily.
● Tie a clean makeshift dressing firmly in place.

If blood still comes through, add more padding and tie more firmly.
    If bleeding from the palm of the hand, put a pad over dressing. Bend fingers over pad to make a fist, and bandage firmly.

Indirect pressure
If direct pressure fails or cannot be properly applied, apply indirect pressure to the relevant artery at a point between the

wound and the heart. Do not exert pressure for more than 15 minutes. Reapply pressure if bleeding continues.
1 Brachial artery: press inner side of upper arm firmly against bone.
2 Femoral artery: bend one knee and use both thumbs – one on top of the other – to press down hard against the pelvic bone in centre of the groin.

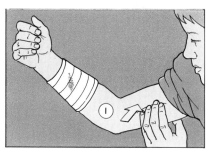

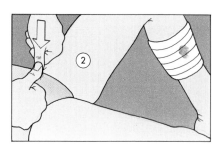

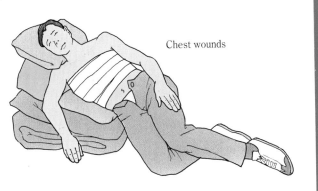

Chest wounds

CHEST WOUNDS
● Put clean pad on wound and press down with the hand to make an airtight seal
● Prop up head and shoulders.
● Lie wounded-side down to ease breathing with remaining good lung.
● Do not remove embedded objects.
● Avoid eating or drinking.

ABDOMINAL WOUNDS
● Lie with shoulders slightly raised, knees bent.
● Cover with anything clean.
● Do not attempt to push any protruding organs back into abdominal cavity.

FOREIGN OBJECTS
● Do not remove any embedded object; it may result in further injury.
● Retain any object used in an attack for forensic evidence.

REMEMBER!
● *Apply pressure to a wound to stop bleeding immediately.*
● *Always try to cover open wound with a clean cloth or pad.*
● *Ring 999 for emergency medical help.*

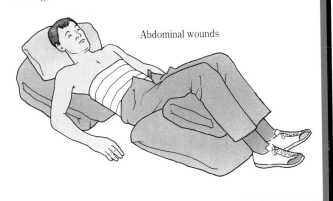

Abdominal wounds

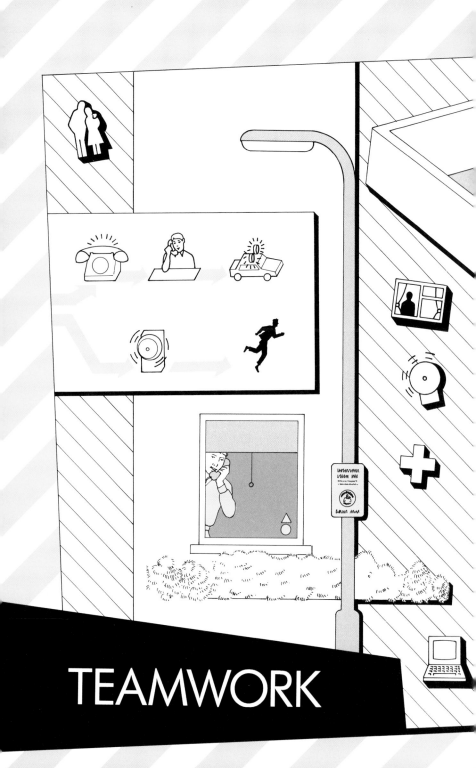

TEAMWORK

TEAMWORK

NEIGHBOURHOOD WATCH

Community Security
HomeWatch
Property Security Marked

TEAMWORK

Preventing crime is everyone's responsibility, and teamwork is the key. By pooling their knowledge and sharing their resources, residents, police, schools, local government, news media and business and industry can play a significant role in increasing public awareness, and in reducing crime and the fear of crime.

The greater the level of local participation, the higher are the chances of reducing burglary, in particular, and even theft, auto crime and assault. In the same way that

THE TEAM

The police
The first priority of the police is to prevent crime. Dealing with the aftermath of crime, and apprehending criminals, is their second priority.

The Home Office
The Home Office carries out research in crime prevention, and produces and distributes literature on crime prevention to the police and the public. Many police forces also produce their own crime prevention literature.

The Home Office Standing Conference on Crime Prevention is an advisory body composed of representatives from local and central government, the police, voluntary organizations, the business community and industry. It examines specific crime problems, and makes recommendations based on its findings.

Local government
Local authorities are increasing their efforts to improve security on housing estates and in the community generally. They may be able to provide:
- Better street lighting.
- Crime prevention literature.
- Grants for the elderly and disabled to fit security devices.

Regulatory and governing bodies
- The British Standards Institute establishes guidelines and minimum requirements for a variety of security products.
- The National Supervisory Council for Intruder Alarms keeps a roll of approved installers, inspects installations, investigates complaints and offers free advice.
- The Association of British Insurers provides advice on home security and on home buildings and contents cover.

Watch schemes
Neighbourhood Watch and Home Watch schemes bring residents into partnership with their local police, and with each other (see pp. 146-9).

Help for victims
- Victims Support Schemes are local voluntary groups that give practical and emotional support to victims of crime in their area (see pp. 150-1).
- Rape Crisis Centres are staffed by female volunteers. They are listed in the telephone directory in cities and larger towns; the national office operates a 24-hour-a-day telephone service to refer callers to the nearest centre (see pp. 162-3).
- The Criminal Injuries Compensation Board can provide financial compensation to victims of violent crime (see pp. 162-3).

small provincial communities traditionally enjoy a relative immunity to serious crime, the creation or re-creation of neighbourhood areas within cities, towns and large suburbs can improve the level of safety and personal security.

YOUR PLACE IN THE TEAM

● The primary responsibility for preventing opportunistic crime rests with you, and *The Personal Security Handbook* shows you how you can do it.

● Get to know your local Crime Prevention Officer, and take advantage of the free security survey he offers.

● Start or join a Neighbourhood Watch scheme (see pp 146-9).

● Work with the local school or with voluntary groups in the community, such as the Victims Support Scheme, Age Concern or Help the Aged, to increase general awareness and reduce the opportunities for crime.

● Work with your community organizations to make local government aware of your area's need for improved street lighting, more public transport, or increased policing.

REMEMBER!
● *Teamwork is the most effective way of reducing crime.*
● *You can help yourself by taking common-sense security precautions.*
● *You can help your community by joining a Watch scheme or other local voluntary group.*
● *You can get help from your Crime Prevention Officer, local authority and voluntary groups in the community.*

THE POLICE

The police are in the front line in the fight against crime. The kinds of crime relevant to personal security – household burglary, auto crime, robbery, theft and assault – comprise a large proportion of their day-to-day workload.

By reducing the opportunities for crime, and by being observant and reporting incidents to the police, you are helping them to work more efficiently.

THE CONSTABULARIES

The police in Britain are organized geographically, in constabularies, and mainly county by county. Each constabulary is an independent police force. It is headed by a Chief Constable, who usually has a deputy and several assistants, and is responsible to the local government authority.

London is an exception. The City of London Police and the Metropolitan Police are each directed by a Commissioner. The Commissioner of the Metropolitan Police is responsible to the Home Secretary.

A constabulary is divided into divisions, each headed by a Chief Superintendent. Depending on the size of the division, there may be several subdivisions, each under the direction of a Superintendent. To provide manpower 24 hours a day, each subdivision is divided into sections.

In rural areas where the police station is a one-man operation, the police officer will vary his hours in the station.

Criminal Investigation Department
The CID in each constabulary is responsible for investigating serious crime, which may range from burglary to homicide. CID officers are attached to every division.

PERSONNEL

Collator
There is a Collator in each division. It is his job to gather information, collate it, and pass it on to the other officers in the division so that they can work more effectively to combat crime. The Collator maintains a crime picture of the area, which helps the Crime Prevention Officer to plan his crime prevention activities and to assess the security precautions you need to take.

Home Beat Officer
The Home Beat Officer is a uniformed policeman or woman assigned to a particular area. He or she will patrol only in that area. If there is a Neighbourhood Watch in that area, the Home Beat Officer will attend Watch meetings and liaise with the Watch coordinator (see pp. 146-9).

THE POLICE

Crime Prevention Officer

There is at least one Crime Prevention Officer (CPO) in each division. He is an experienced policeman who has been selected because of his knowledge of how criminals work. He is specially trained in crime prevention techniques, the technicalities of security hardware and electronic equipment, and in skilled communication. Once appointed to that job, a CPO is not involved in other aspects of police duty, except in emergencies.

In most instances you come into contact with your local CPO only when he conducts a security survey of your home. However, his duties extend far beyond this. He also:

● Conducts security surveys on industrial and commercial premises, and advises on measures to prevent crimes ranging from burglary to terrorism.

● Gives talks on crime prevention or specific local crime problems on the radio and to organizations such as Residents' Associations, Parent-Teacher Associations, local Chambers of Commerce and Retailers Associations.

● Gives talks to individual companies on specific aspects of crime prevention, such as how to prevent shoplifting.

● Organizes the distribution of crime prevention publicity material.

● Initiates and manages crime prevention campaigns to publicize and alleviate local crime problems.

● Organizes exhibitions in his area to publicize the concept of crime prevention and to provide on-the-spot consultation and advice to local residents.

● Is a member of, and provides guidance and advice to, crime prevention panels.

CRIME PREVENTION PANELS

These panels are another example of teamwork in the fight against crime. Each panel comprises police officers and representatives of the local community.

The police on the panel may include a senior officer, a CID officer and the Crime Prevention Officer.

The object is to have a broad cross-section of the community on the panel. It usually includes representatives of the local government authority, local churches, commerce, press, transport services, education, and youth workers.

The panel meets regularly to try to alleviate crime problems within its area.

REMEMBER!

● *You can help the police to prevent crime.*

● *The Crime Prevention Officer provides free and impartial advice on security for your home.*

NEIGHBOURHOOD WATCH 1

In the early 1970s communities in the United States began to form voluntary organizations to combat the increasing number of burglaries. Known as the Neighbourhood Watch, these schemes achieved a remarkable reduction not only in the number of burglaries, but also in street crime, auto crime and vandalism. Their success led police forces in Britain and many other countries to develop similar Neighbourhood Watch schemes to meet local needs.

WHAT IT IS

A Neighbourhood Watch, Home Watch, Crime Watch, or other similarly named scheme consists of residents in a particular locality who form a group to help prevent burglary and other types of crime within that area.

The Watch may be initiated by the residents, the police or both. In all cases it is advised by, and works in close cooperation with, the local police.

HOW IT WORKS

EYES AND EARS

Everyone resident in the defined area is encouraged to be a member of the Watch. As a participant in a scheme, you are expected to be particularly observant as you go about your daily routine, and to be on the look-out for crime or any suspicious behaviour that might result in a crime taking place in the Watch area. However, you are not expected to, and should not, patrol the streets actively looking for suspicious situations to report.

If you see people acting suspiciously around local homes, schools, shops, or even vehicles, you pass that information to the police immediately. You should not become involved in any way with a suspected criminal – that is the job of the police, and best left to them.

Coordinators

The scheme is run by the members, in liaison with the police. There need to be people to coordinate the work of the members and to be responsible for the two-way flow of non-urgent information between them and the local police.

There are coordinators in every street or block of flats. They:
● Keep in touch with all the members, providing support and encouragement.
● Hold meetings to keep members well-informed and in touch with each other.
● Recruit new members.
● Help with property marking.
● Deliver the newsletter.

The area coordinator maintains daily contact with the street coordinators and the police. He may arrange meetings at which all the street coordinators can discuss the problems or progress in their street and receive more advice from the police as necessary.

CRIME PREVENTION SURVEY

Each member of a scheme is given the opportunity of a free crime prevention survey by the local Crime Prevention Officer. He will advise you on the security hardware you need to keep the burglar out of your home.

PROPERTY MARKING

Like every member of the Watch, you are expected to mark your property (see pp. 62-3) to deter burglars, as well as to help in identifying property that has been stolen.

Although this is an essential part of a Watch scheme, you should, of course, also mark your property even if you don't belong to a Watch group.

NEIGHBOURHOOD WATCH 1

Window stickers
In most Watch areas the local police force supplies window stickers. One advertises the fact that the occupant of the house is a member of the Watch. The other tells the burglar that property in the house has been uniquely marked and is identifiable. Both are deterrents to the potential burglar.

Street signs
Street signs stating that 'You are entering a Watch area' may be erected on lamp posts around the perimeter of the area, but should be placed high enough to prevent vandalism. They deter the potential burglar because he knows that in that area eyes and ears will be looking and listening for him, that the houses will be properly secured, and that the goods worth stealing will be marked.

THE NEWSLETTER
The newsletter may be produced by the police or by members of the Watch. The information in it is supplied by the police and includes:
● Trends in crime.
● Criminal tactics.
● Descriptions of suspects.
● Tips on crime prevention.

REMEMBER!
● *A local Watch scheme can help to reduce crime and the fear of crime.*
● *Members of a Watch scheme need to be observant and neighbourly.*
● *It is your responsibility to deter crime.*
● *It is the job of the police to prevent crime and catch criminals.*

ENVIRONMENTAL IMPROVEMENT

There are a number of environmental factors that might affect the incidence of crime in an area, such as street lighting, the siting of bus stops, or unofficial rubbish dumps.
    The Watch liaises with the local authority to make improvements.

NEIGHBOURHOOD WATCH 2

SETTING UP A NEIGHBOURHOOD WATCH SCHEME

Many Watch schemes are successful in helping to reduce burglary and other crime in their area. In this way they increase the quality of life for all the residents. They improve the public's relationship with the local police and result in better and more effective communication between them.

Schemes initiated by the police

Each police force has its own policy on setting up Neighbourhood Watch schemes – and there may still be a few forces who do not have any schemes in their area. The example that follows, therefore, is a general outline of how a scheme might be set up, not a detailed plan of how your local force might do it.

The police will usually try to set up a scheme in an area with a high incidence of burglary, in order to combat the problem. Of course, a Watch scheme can be started and maintained only with the cooperation of the local residents. If, for any reason, they do not want a Neighbourhood Watch in their area, the police cannot impose one.

For this reason the police will canvass the locality first to see how much support there is for a scheme. They may send a questionnaire to every household or call on each one individually. If a representative body, such as a residents' association, already exists, the police might approach this first.

If the enquiries indicate that there will be sufficient support for a Watch, the police will arrange a meeting with the community to explain how the scheme works. In addition to local residents, the meeting will be attended by a senior police officer, the local Crime Prevention Officer and the Home Beat Officer (see pp. 144-5).

The police will explain how the scheme works, and what members are expected to do and not to do. They will suggest that street coordinators and an area co-ordinator be elected.

A second meeting may then be arranged. In the interim the coordinators and members of the Watch can get acquainted and recruit new members.

At the second meeting the police will review how the scheme works and instruct members on how to recognize suspicious behaviour, how to record descriptions of suspects, and how to mark property.

Schemes initiated by the public

If the members of a community decide that they want a Neighbourhood Watch in their area, they approach their local police to help them set it up.

In most cases, the police will want a Watch to consist of a minimum number of members to make their support worthwhile. Therefore, if you are thinking of proposing a Watch in your area, ask your local police how many participants you need to make the scheme viable.

When you have gathered a sufficient number of interested people, the police will proceed to help you set up a scheme in the way described above.

Watch schemes also encourage a community spirit, replacing what might have been social isolation for many people in the neighbourhood in large urban centres.

WHAT THE POLICE NEED TO KNOW

As a member of a Watch, the police need you to provide the following information.

Description of a suspicious person
● Male or female.
● Colour of skin.
● Complexion.
● Height.
● Build.
● Probable age.
● Hair; colour; length; straight or curly; receding or bald.
● Eyes: colour; glasses.
● Face: long; thin; cleanshaven; moustache; beard.
● Marks: scars; tatoos; birthmarks.
● Mouth: wide; full; narrow.
● Style and colour of clothing and shoes.

Description of a suspicious vehicle
● Type of vehicle: car; van, lorry, motorbike.
● Make and model.
● Colour.
● Body type.
● Registration number.
● Other details: damage, stickers, company name or advertising.
● Where it was parked.
● The direction in which it travelled.

Maintenance of schemes
Most police forces have some sort of programme to maintain the initial impetus of a Watch.

From time to time, they may hold meetings for the Watch at which the Crime Prevention Officer, the Home Beat Officer, or a CID officer may address the members on a specific topic relating to crime problems in the area.

They will supply information about crime problems – and progress in prevention and solution of crimes – for the Watch newsletter. In some cases, the police may even produce the newsletter.

REMEMBER!
● *You can help the police by being observant.*
● *Report suspicious behaviour to the police immediately.*
● *If your report is urgent, dial 999. Otherwise, ring your local police station.*

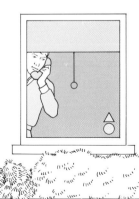

VICTIMS SUPPORT SCHEMES

Victims Support Schemes provide first-aid for the practical and emotional problems experienced by the victim of a crime, which fall outside the scope of the police and social services.

The effects of crime are unexpected and disruptive, materially and psychologically. They require immediate attention, and sometimes continuing care, to prevent long-lasting distress. An experienced and

HOW IT WORKS

The Victims Support Scheme (VSS) deals with the victims of all types of crime. It makes every effort to contact the victims as soon as possible after the crime has been reported, and to help him or her return to a normal way of life. The service is provided by local volunteers, and is free and confidential. A VSS group consists of a management committee, a coordinator and volunteer visitors.

THE MANAGEMENT COMMITTEE
The committee must include representatives from the:
● Local police.
● Social services or probation service.
● Local voluntary organization, such as the Citizens' Advice Bureau or church.
● Volunteer visitors.

It may also include representatives from local business, trade, professional or other community organizations, experienced members of other VSS groups, and interested individuals.

THE COORDINATOR
The coordinator contacts the police daily for the names of people who have been the victims of crime during the past 24 hours. He or she passes the information to one of the volunteer visitors.

THE VOLUNTEERS
The volunteers who visit the victims of crime are members of the local community. They are trained to:
● Listen to the victims.
● Evaluate their needs.
● Comfort those who are in need of emotional support.
● Act where practical help is required.
● Make referrals to appropriate agencies for further assistance.

Immediate response
The volunteer will try to call on the victim the day he or she receives the referral. If the volunteer can't contact the victim initially, he or she leaves or sends a letter. Victims can also contact the VSS direct.

On his or her first visit (women rape victims are always seen by a woman) the visitor encourages the victim or members of the household to talk about the crime and their feelings as much as they need to. He also evaluates the situation and offers whatever advice or practical help is needed. He may visit a victim once or twice, or maintain regular contact until the end of the court case.

Practical help
The volunteer can give the victim practical help with:
● Making insurance claims.
● Getting damaged or broken locks, doors or windows repaired or replaced.
● Clearing up household disorder.
● Getting stolen documents, such as pension books and bus passes, replaced.
● Caring for dependants.
● Arranging re-housing.
● Contacting other specialist services.
● Improving home security.

sympathetic person to talk to, who can provide reassurance, and who will help to get locks replaced, report the loss of important documents, or even tidy up the home after a messy burglary can be invaluable.

VICTIMS SUPPORT SCHEMES

Emotional support
The volunteer can provide useful emotional support by:
● Being a good listener.
● Comforting those in need.
● Taking enough time to let the victim feel valued.
● Restoring the victim's faith in society, by showing that although one stranger may have damaged his or her life, another is trying to help.
● Accompanying the victim to identity parades or court.

REMEMBER!
● *The Victims Support Scheme helps victims of all types of crime.*
● *The service is free and confidential.*
● *You can help your local VSS by contributing your time, skills, or money.*
● *To find out where your local scheme is, aks your local police or Citizens' Advice Bureau, or the National Association of Victims Support Schemes (see pp. 162-3).*

THE NATIONAL ASSOCIATION OF VICTIMS SUPPORT SCHEMES

● Maintains a code of practice to ensure high standards in member schemes.
● Provides local schemes with administrative and publicity materials.
● Coordinates the sharing of knowledge and experience between member schemes.
● Develops specific areas of relevant study .

● Functions as a press and information office, and a focal point for facilities and funding.
● Is committed to crime prevention initiatives and reducing the fear of crime.
● Provides Victims Support with a national platform.
● Is financed by a Home Office grant augmented by voluntary contributions.

HOW YOU CAN HELP
● Become a volunteer visitor.
● Take part in management or fund-raising activities.
● Offer your practical skills or professional expertise.
● Make a donation; the National Association of Victims Support Schemes is a registered charity.

YOU are a WITNESS

Anyone at any time, anywhere, may witness a crime. You might think you would be incapable of remembering anything about such a dramatic incident once it is over, whether it is a bank robbery or a snatched handbag in the street. The speed with which the crime occurs might also make it difficult to remember any details.

However, if you know what kind of information the police hope a witness will be able to provide, you will be the better able to cope with the situation.

Being a witness can be divided into three distinct stages:
1 Witnessing the crime;
2 Helping the police;
3 Appearing at court

WITNESSING THE CRIME

You are walking along the High Street in your local shopping area. As you are approaching a bank, you see two men run out of the door; one is carrying a sawn-off shotgun and the other has a revolver. Both are wearing stocking masks. They pull off the masks as they jump into a car waiting at the kerb, and drive away at high speed.

You are in a position to pass a valuable amount of information to the police if you can mentally note and remember it. If you have a pen and paper with you, make notes as soon as you can, particularly the vehicle registration number.

Never assume that somebody else has called the police; if you're not absolutely sure, ring 999 yourself. Wait for the police to arrive and give them as much of the following information as you can.

The crime
● The exact time the crime took place.
● The precise location at which the crime occurred.

The vehicle
● The make, model and colour, and any distinguishing features, such as damage or window stickers.
● The registration number.
● The direction in which it went.
● The number of people in it.

The robbers
Try to remember as much as possible about each one separately, and about anyone else you noticed in the car, particularly:
● Height.
● Build.
● Complexion.
● Shape of face.
● Colour and style (moustache, beard) of any facial hair.
● Length, style and colour of head hair.
● Scars, tattoos or other distinguishing features on the face or hands.
● The colour and style of clothing: coats, jackets, jumpers, trousers and shoes.
● Jewellery, such as chains, watches, earrings, rings.
● Description of the firearms.
● Anything said by either of them, especially any name used.
● Type of voice – gruff, high-pitched – and accent.

HELPING THE POLICE

After the police have completed their initial investigation at the scene of the crime, they will ask you to go to the police station to make a statement. A detective will take your statement, guiding you through it step by step to help you focus your memory accurately.

You may be asked to help a specialist prepare an identikit picture of each of the robbers. You may also be shown photographs and asked if the men who took part in the robbery are among them.

Some time later you might be asked to go to the police station again to attend an identification parade. You will see a line of at least eight men, and be asked if any of them are recognizable as the men who took part in the robbery.

APPEARING AT COURT

You will have to attend court to give evidence only if the defendants contest the charge. A case of this seriousness will be heard in a Crown Court before a judge and jury. The counsels for the prosecution and the defence will have copies of the statement you made to the police.

The counsel for the prosecution will ask you questions to elicit your evidence. The counsel for the defence will then cross-examine you. The prosecuting counsel may ask you a few more questions to clear up any points that might have arisen. You will then be free to leave. You have been a witness.

ASSAULT

If you witness an assault, don't intervene unless you are absolutely sure you can spare the victim and protect yourself from the assailant. You may help the victim more by summoning the police.

If there is an evenly matched fight, it is possible that both combatants will attack anyone who tries to interfere.

THE VICTIM

If you are the victim of a crime, you will have to appear in court only if the defendant enters a plea of not guilty.

The procedures in court will be the same as those described for the witness to a crime.

If you are the victim of a burglary and the defendant pleads guilty, you do not need to go to court.

However, you will be asked by the police to identify any of your stolen property that has been recovered, and to state that on the day the incident occurred no one had the authority to enter your home while it was unoccupied.

This information will be recorded in a formal statement.

YOU are a WITNESS

REMEMBER!
If you witness a crime
- *Try to stay calm.*
- *Dial 999.*
- *Make notes about what you have seen.*

THE FUTURE

Preventing crime is everyone's responsibility. By implementing the simple precautions illustrated in *The Personal Security Handbook,* you can effectively prevent opportunistic crime and make the future safer for yourself and your family.

On the larger scale, steady advances in technology will increase the sophistication of security products, improve the rate and speed of detection of criminals, and

HOME SAFE

Computerized home security systems will become standard.
Homes will be protected by a comprehensive system that can:
● Detect intruders as well as smoke;
● Automatically operate every electrical device, from lights to personal panic alarms;
● Send an electronic call for help.

VEHICLE SECURITY

Cars will be manufactured to meet new British Standards for:
● Window etching and the quality of glazing.
● The protection of entertainment units (radio/cassette players).
● Production-line alarm systems and central or power door-locking systems.

THE WARY TRAVELLER

● Security screening at airports will include sealing all inspected luggage with special tape, so no one will be able to tamper with your bags and baggage undetected.

● Computerized hotel room keys will become standard in new buildings. Even if you lose your key or it is stolen, without the unique code, no one can use it to enter your room. It is reprogrammed for each new visitor.

TEAMWORK

Computerizing the police

Advances in computer technology will increase the speed with which stored data can be accessed and correlated.
This will continue to have a tremendous impact on police efficiency in crime solving and resource deployment.
● Crime detection will be revolutionized by the introduction of high-speed automatic fingerprint recognition (AFR).

AFR will hold the entire national collection of prints on computer. Every force will have a direct computer link with the archive, and be able to compare the fingerprints on record with those lifted from the scene of the crime, or taken from individuals.
● Future technology will enable prints to be taken from all types of surface, rough or smooth – even from clothing or a victim's skin.
● The AFR system will also include 'genetic fingerprints'.

The unique gene structure of body fluids (such as blood, perspiration or semen), which may be found at the scene of a crime or on a victim, is as distinctive as a fingerprint. The police can use it to identify an individual in the same way.
● Photographic retrieval from optical disc (PROD) will provide high-speed access to 'mug shots'.
The system will search files for an image to match the description given by a witness.

If a match can be made, seconds later the computer's visual display unit will show a named person's face in colour, and a laser printer will instantly produce black and white copies for witnesses to check.
● The police will use PROD to amass visual files on the *modus operandi* of criminals. This more refined information narrows the field witnesses are obliged to go through. Further, since only about one in five criminals are repeat offenders within a given force area, PROD would make sorting them out far easier.

advance the gathering and sharing of crime prevention information. Some of the main improvements in personal security are predicted below.

PERSONAL SECURITY

- An awareness of potentially dangerous situations and common sense in avoiding them will continue to be the guidelines for personal safety.

- Developing a positive and self-confident attitude, plus an understanding of basic self-defence techniques, will free more people from the fear of crime.

- Personal alarms will be refined to enhance their convenience and reliabiity.

  Those designed for the particular needs of the elderly will allow greater independence and freedom from worry, both at home and out and about, as monitoring facilities are expanded.

THE FUTURE

REMEMBER!
- *Common-sense precautions will continue to be the best way to prevent crime.*
- *Taking measures to prevent crime also reduces the fear of crime.*
- *Preventing crime is* your *responsibility.*

- Police officers on the street will have access to stored information with portable slimline terminals linked to computer records.
- Forensic science will use portable compact laser units at the scenes of crimes to collect elusive prints and other evidence.
- In police stations, high-quality video recordings of interviews will be standard.
- Computers will improve the ability of local forces to analyse problem areas on a weekly basis so that they can allocate their resources according to the shifting pattern.

Private enterprise
- Manufacturers of security products will continue to develop more sophisticated deterrents.
- The British Security Industries Association has sponsored a crime prevention competition, seeking original ideas from the public as well as from manufacturers.
  Design Against Crime winners are advised on patenting and marketing their inventions.

Winning designs have included an effective cycle rack, a tamper-proof letterbox and a new-generation trap alarm for those individual items of electrical equipment that top the home burglar's shopping list.

Victims
- Greater emphasis will be placed on victims' needs and rights, and on the importance of integrating their experiences into an overall campaign against crime.

APPENDICES

GLOSSARY

Access control: means by which only authorized persons are allowed to enter a building or flat and unauthorized persons kept out.

All-risks coverage: insurance for items taken out of the home, including cash, and for individually specified items of value.

Arming: means by which an alarm system is switched on; may be manual, passive or remote control.

Audio entry system: a means of access control in which a speaker panel outside the premises is linked to a telephone handset inside and a remote-control button that releases the electrically operated door lock.

Audio-visual entry system: an audio entry system with the addition of closed circuit television (CCTV).

Audio warning device: means by which an alarm system sounds the alarm, usually a bell or siren; also called signal.

Automated dialling equipment (ADE): alarm system that sends a recorded message on an ex-directory line to the telephone exchange to be relayed to the police.

Auto crime: any crime involving a motor vehicle.

Break-glass detector: sensor responsive to sound frequencies emitted by breaking plate glass.

Buildings coverage: insurance for the fabric of a building and its permanent internal and external fixtures and fittings.

Burglary: the unlawful entering of the home of another person with the intention of stealing, and/or stealing therefrom.

Burglary by artifice: burglary that is perpetrated by a person who gains access to the home by misrepresenting himself to the occupant.

Common assault: assault or attempted assault in which injury is negligible or nonexistent.

Contents coverage: insurance for household goods and personal property within the home.

Contact switch: in vehicle and household alarm systems, a magnetic or electrical device located on doors and windows to detect entry or tampering.

Control: the part of a system that arms and disarms the alarm, activates the warning in response to detectors, and checks the circuit for faults.

Deadlock: a bolt that can be withdrawn into the lockcase only by a key.

Detection zone: range over which an alarm detector is effective.

Detector: the scanning and screening device in an alarm system that identifies tampering or entry and signals the control.

Digital communicator: alarm system that sends coded signal on ex-directory line to the security company's central station.

Digital lock: electronic lock that can be opened only by keying in appropriate number code.

Direct private wire: alarm signal transmitted on continuously monitored private line to security company's central control station.

Disabler switch: means of immobilizing vehicle by interrupting ignition feed wire.

Disarming: means by which an alarm system is switched off.

Door chain: removable chain fitted to the inside of the door frame to limit the opening to a few inches so that callers may be safely identified.

Door limiter: similar to a door chain, but using a sliding-rod device.

Door viewer: a small lens installed in the door at eye level to enable the occupant to see out.

Earth-seeking sensor: vehicle alarm system pin-switch or door contact that is activated when the electrical current is broken.

Espagnolette bolt: two vertical bolts covering top and bottom halves of a door, connected and operated by a central lock.

Exclusions: the items an insurance policy does not cover, or conditions that invalidate cover.

External alarm: an alarm set in the grounds to detect intruders before the shell of the house is breached.

Face plate: the visible part of a lock on the leading edge of the door.

Fitch catch: a pivoting device used to lock the top and bottom panes of a sash window together.

Forcible entry: unauthorized entry of a secured dwelling or vehicle, usually causing damage.

Geophone: vibration-monitoring device used to detect activity across the ground or along walls and fences.

Green Card: temporary policy rider extending car insurance coverage when a vehicle is taken abroad.

Grille: a fixed, sliding or hinged metal barrier to protect glazed areas of doors and windows.

Hasp: hinged flap through which staple is slotted for securing by padlock.

Hinged bolts: small metal rods fixed on the hinge edge of the door, which fit into corresponding holes in the frame when the door is closed to prevent the door from being forced open or lifted.

Hitch lock: a device that locks into the socket of a vehicle-towing hitch to prevent unauthorized use.

Horizontal curtain: trap alarm using horizontally aligned passive infra-red (PIR) monitoring to detect a break-in through roof, ceiling or floor.

Household insurance: cover comprised of buildings, contents and all-risks.

Indecent assault: the touching of another person's sexual organs without his or her consent.

Independent audio warning: in vehicle alarms, a siren or hooter that is not powered by the car's electrical system.

Index-linking: in household insurance policies, automatic monthly updating of sums insured in line with the House Rebuilding Cost Index (buildings) and the Retail Price Index (contents).

Infra-red beam detector: a device that signals an alarm when an invisible beam between its projector and receiver is broken.

Integral garage: one attached to the house and linked by an internal door.

Ionization detector: type of smoke alarm that reacts to excess carbon particles in the air.

Laminated glass: safety glass that cracks but does not break under impact.

Lock case: the portion of the lock set into the door's edge, into which the bolt is withdrawn for opening.

Locking plate: portion of the lock fitted into the frame of the door, into which the bolt passes when locked.

Locking stile: upright portion of door, also called leading edge, into which the locking plate fits.

Loss adjuster: person sent by insurance company to recommend figure for settlement on a claim.

Loss assessor: person who may be hired by policy holder to give a second opinion when disputing the figure suggested by the insurer for settlement.

Magnetic reed contact: alarm system detection device in which a disruption of the magnetic field between two points causes a break in the electrical current and signals the control to activate the alarm.

Microwave fence: external alarm that signals the alarm when beams of invisible microwaves between transmitter and receiver are disturbed.

GLOSSARY

Microwave movement detector: trap alarm with single-unit transmitter/receiver that reacts to distortions in the timing of its return signal.

Monitoring: the control function of an alarm system that checks detection circuits for damage or tampering before setting. Also refers to continuous checking of a direct wire against damage or tampering in a direct private wire system.

Mortise bolt: a deadlocking bolt fitted into a recess cut in the locking stile of the door.

Mortise latch-lock: mortise lock incorporating a latch and handle.

Mortise lock: a lock that fits into a recess cut in the locking stile of the door, operated by key only.

Motion detector: sensor that reacts to movement, such as a car being jacked up, rocked or towed.

Mugging: an unofficial term popularly used to describe violent street robbery and snatch-theft.

Natural surveillance: extent to which a house or point of entry is clearly visible to casual observers.

Neighbourhood Watch: crime prevention scheme that emphasizes neighbourly observation and responsibility, run by residents in liaison with the local police.

Night latch: a spring lock that can be opened from the inside without a key and cannot be deadlocked.

Notifiable offences: offences recorded by the police and used in compiling official criminal statistics.

Opportunist crime: unplanned, spontaneous crime taking advantage of favourable conditions.

Panic button: deliberately operated alarm, worn on the person or installed in a suitable place inside the home; remains on permanently.

Passive arming: vehicle alarm system that activates automatically when you leave the car.

Passive infra-red (PIR) detector: device that receives and measures infra-red energy from other objects.

Patio door lock: security device that bolts sliding door to frame.

Perimeter: the enclosed or unenclosed boundary of a property; the first point of trespass.

Perimeter alarm: one protecting the shell of the building – walls, doors, windows.

Perimeter barrier: wall, fence or gate marking the perimeter of the property.

Photo-electric detector: smoke detector that is activated when its light beam is disturbed.

Physical deterrents: locks, bolts and other physical means of discourging unauthorized entry.

Points of entry: doors, windows and other openings providing access to the interior of a building, flat or vehicle.

Premium: the sum paid for insurance cover.

Pre-set exit and entry: alarm control feature that allows a prescribed period of time to leave and re-enter the home or car without setting off the alarm.

Pressure mat: detector that responds to weight on it; usually concealed under carpet and used as perimeter or trap alarm.

Property Irregularity Report (PIR): document completed at your request and in your presence by air, shipping, coach or rail carrier when you report loss of, or damage to, property.

Property marking: coding of property by ultraviolet pen, etching or die-stamping to deter theft and to facilitate the recovery of stolen goods.

Psychological deterrents: wide range of mainly visual disincentives to the criminal to pursue his target; includes alarms, warning signs, natural surveillance, watch dog.

Rape: unlawful sexual intercourse with a person against his or her consent and induced by fear, force or fraud.

Registered key: a key that can be duplicated or replaced by the manufacturer only on production of the owner's signature.

Remote control arming/disarming: use of radio or infra-red signal to switch an alarm system on and off, usually with a hand-held unit.

Remote control lock: one activated by an infra-red beam from a hand-held device.

Remote signalling device: the part of an alarm system that sends a message by telephone to the security company's central control station.

Rim deadlock: deadlock fitted to the inside surface of the door.

Robbery: theft of property directly from a person accompanied by violence or the threat violence at the time of, or immediately preceding, the taking.

Shell: the walls of the home; second point of trespass.

Security key switch: external device allowing manual arming and disarming of vehicle alarm system.

Security lock: high-quality lock for which duplicate keys cannot be obtained without authorization. Can have a high security lock without key registration.

Signal: action taken when household or vehicle alarm system is activated; usually audio warning, such as bell or siren.

Stile: upright piece of door to which a lock or hinge is fitted.

Striking plate: metal plate, preferably incorporating a box to defend against jemmy attack, into which a bolt shoots when extended.

Surface bolt: bolt screwed horizontally or vertically onto the surface of a door, window or gate, which shoots into a staple on the locking frame, top frame, floor or sill.

Target hardening: use of security hardware to protect property against intruders.

Tempered glass: heat-toughened safety glass that shatters into pieces with no sharp edges.

Theft: unlawful taking of a person's property without his consent and with the intention to deprive him of it permanently.

Theft from a motor vehicle: taking of any personal property or accessories in or on a vehicle.

Theft of motor vehicle: vehicle taken without the consent of the owner and not recovered within one month.

Theft from the person: unlawful taking of property directly from a person without his consent, but without violence; usually refers to pocket-picking or handbag snatching.

Trap alarm: detection device installed within the home to detect an intruder after entry; may be used to protect individual items.

Ultrasonic movement detector: single-unit transmitter/receiver that signals an alarm when its steady pattern of inaudible sound waves is disturbed.

Unlawful taking of a motor vehicle: when a vehicle is taken without the consent of the owner, but is recovered within one month.

Valuation: amount for which property is insured.

Vandalism: willful damage to property.

Vibration detector: sensor placed on walls to register vibration caused by blows or drilling.

Window etching: permanent security coding of car windows and headlamp glass to deter theft.

ADDRESSES

Many of the following organizations have a very wide range of activities, but the way in which they are relevant to personal security is explained briefly under the address.

● National headquarters: will refer you to relevant local organization.

●● Governing body: will supply list of members.

HOME SAFE

●● **Association of British Insurers,** Aldermary House, 10-15 Queen Street, London EC4N 1TV. Tel: 01-248-4477
Free advice on insurance matters; leaflets on home security and household cover.

●● **British Security Industries Association,** Scorpio House, 102 Sydney Street, London SW3 6NL. Tel: 01-352-8219
Free list of approved safe, lock and alarm manufacturers and installers that meet or exceed British Standards.

British Standards Institute, 2 Park Street, London W1. Tel: 01-629-9000
National body responsible for drafting and publishing British Standards, and for testing and certifying products that meet those standards. Approved products bear an official BS number and 'kite' mark.

Fire Protection Association, 140 Aldersgate Street, London EC1A 4HX. Tel: 01-606-3757
Free advice and brochures on fire prevention and safety.

●● **Glass and Glazing Federation,** 44-48 Borough High Street, London SE1 1XP. Tel: 01-403-7177
Free advice on all aspects of safety glass and double glazing; free list of approved manufacturers (written enquiries preferred).

●● **Institute of Public Loss Assessors,** 14 Red Lion Street, Chesham, Buckinghamshire HP5 1HB. Tel: 0494-782342
Free list of loss assessors.

● **The Kennel Club,** 1-4 Clarges Street, London W1Y 8AB. Tel: 01-493-6651
Free lists of approved breed clubs and local dog-training clubs.

●● **National Supervisory Council for Intruder Alarms,** St Ives House, St Ives Road, Maidenhead, Berkshire SL6 1RD. Tel: 0628-37512
Free list of approved manufacturers and installers that comply with BS 4737 and the NSCIA Code of Practice.

Royal Society for the Prevention of Accidents, Cannon House, The Priory, Queensway, Birmingham B4 6BS. Tel: 021-233-2461
Free information on various aspects of home safety.

VEHICLE SECURITY

See *Home Safe:* Association of British Insurers; British Standards Institute.

THE WARY TRAVELLER

See *Home Safe:* Association of British Insurers.

PERSONAL SAFETY/TEAMWORK

● **Age Concern England,** 60 Pitcairn Road, Mitcham, Surrey CR4 3LL. Tel: 01-640-5431
Includes crime prevention information in its work with the elderly and in its publications.

● **British Red Cross Society,** 9 Grosvenor Crescent, London SW1X 7EJ. Tel: 01-235-5454
Gives training in first aid.

Criminal Injuries Compensation Board, Whittington House, 19 Alfred Place, London WC1E 7LG. Tel: 01-639-9501
Provides financial compensation to some victims of violent crime.

● **Help the Aged,** St James Walk, London EC1R 0BE. Tel: 01-250-3399
Provides security advice to the elderly.

Kidscape, 82 Brook Street, London W1Y 1YG. Tel: 01-493-9845
Free information pack designed for those in charge of children to help the young ward off the advances of strangers.

- **National Association for the Care and Rehabilitation of Offenders (NACRO),** 169 Clapham Road, London SW9 0PU. Tel: 01-582-6500
Involves former criminals in constructive anti-crime activities.

- **National Association of Victims Support Schemes,** 17A Electric Avenue, London SW9 8LA. Tel: 01-326-1084
Coordinates local member groups offering practical and emotional help to victims of crime.

- **National Women's Aid Federation,** 52-54 Featherstone Street, London EC1Y 8RT. 01-251-6537
Help and information for women and children victims of domestic violence.

- **Rape Crisis Centre/24-hour referral,** PO Box 69, London WC1. Tel: 01-837-1600/021-233-2122
Refers callers to nearest Rape Crisis Centre, where advice and assistance is provided by experienced female volunteers.

- **St Andrew's Ambulance Association,** St Andrew's House, Milton Street, Glasgow G4 0HR. Tel: 041-332-4031
Provides first aid training in Scotland.

- **St John Ambulance,** 1 Grosvenor Crescent, London SW1X 7EF. Tel: 01-235-5231
Offers first aid training in England and Wales; publishes first aid handbook.

PUBLICATIONS

Her Majesty's Stationery Office
The official government publisher. Publications include Laws, Acts, Criminal Statistics and the British Crime Survey. Bookshops in major towns throughout the country; consult local listings or the *Guide to HMSO Publications and Services,* available from:
Publicity Department, HMSO Books, St Crispins, Duke Street, Norwich NR3 1PD. Tel: 0603-622211

HMSO Book Orders, PO Box 276, London SW8. Tel: 01-622-3316
Takes telephone orders for HMSO publications.
Security Publications Limited, Argosy House, 161A-163A High Street, Orpington, Kent BR6 0LW. Tel: 0689-74025
Publishes the quarterly magazine *Good Neighbour,* available on subscription to Neighbourhood Watch and Home Watch members.

AUSTRALIA

National Safety Council of Australia (NSCA), 370 St. Kilda Road, Melbourne, Victoria 3004. Tel: (03)-690-2300
Publications *Australian Safety News, Australian Family Safety.*
Safety Institute of Australia, Inc, 104 South Parade, Blackburn, Victoria 3130. Tel: (03)-878-1774
Australian Insurance Institute, 31 Queen Street, Melbourne, Victoria 3000. Tel: (03)-62-4021
Australian Red Cross Society, 206 Clarendon Street, East Melbourne, Victoria 3002. Tel: (03)-419-7533
National Council of Women of Australia, 24 McGregor Street, Clayfield, Queensland 4011
National Crime Authority, Central Office, G.P.O. Box 5260, Sydney, New South Wales 2001. Tel: (02)-265-7111. Melbourne Office: G.P.O. Box 238E, Melbourne, Victoria 3001.
Australian Crime Prevention Council, P.O. Box 147, Broadbeach, Queensland 4127. Tel: (075)-35-5327
Australian Federal Police (AFP), Police Headquarters, NRMA House, 92 Northbourne Avenue, Braddon, A.C.T. 2601. Tel: (062)-49-7444
Department of Community Services, 333 Kent Street, Sydney, New South Wales 2000; G.P.O. Box 4292, Sydney, NSW 2001. Tel: (02)-225-3555
Australian Government Publishing Service, G.P.O. Box 84, Canberra, A.C.T. 2601.

INDEX

INDEX

INDEX